How to Survive Personal Bankruptcy

in England & Wales

Lee Betteridge

Published in Great Britain by Lee Betteridge
34 Oak Crescent, Garforth, Leeds, West Yorkshire, LS25 1PN
www.survivebankruptcy.info

A CIP catalogue record for this book is available from the British Library

ISBN 978-0-9562051-0-0

Printed in Great Britain by the MPG Books Group,
Bodmin and King's Lynn
First Printing June 2009

Cover design and preparation for print by John F Griffiths © 2009
www.e-griff.com

Disclaimer

This book provides general information only and does not constitute professional advice. While a great deal of care has been taken to ensure that the information is accurate and current, it is not a full and authoritative statement of the law and you should not rely on it as such. The reader is therefore urged to seek legal advice regarding points of law.

Furthermore, the publisher makes no representations or warranties with respect to the accuracy or completeness of the contents of this work. The information contained herein may not be suitable for every situation. Where professional assistance is required, the services of a competent professional person should be sought.

It should be noted that the information in this book is applicable to England and Wales only. If you are unsure whether you qualify to file for bankruptcy in England and Wales you should call the Insolvency Service Enquiry Line on 0845 602 9848 to obtain further guidance.

The fact that an organisation or website is referred to in this work, as a potential source of further information, does not mean that the publisher endorses the information that the organisation or website may provide, or recommendations it may make.

Dedication

This book is dedicated to my family, especially my mother, and to the memory of my grandparents. It is also dedicated to anyone currently experiencing financial difficulties. It is my sincere hope that you discover the appropriate guidance and support to help you on your way to a happy and healthy debt-free future.

Acknowledgement

I would like to extend my deepest gratitude and thanks to John Griffiths for his invaluable help in editing and laying out the book and cover. I thank him for his professionalism, commitment and patience.

Contents

Part IV: While You Are Undischarged

Part V: After You Are Discharged

Introduction

The fact that you are reading this book means that you, or someone you know, are probably in some kind of financial difficulty. Maybe you have already been made bankrupt, or perhaps you haven't yet decided whether bankruptcy is the right solution for you. You may even be discharged from bankruptcy and looking to take the first positive steps into a future free from debt.

Every case is unique, but whatever your current situation, it is of huge importance that you have access to the right information. This book has been written from the perspective of someone who has been through the whole bankruptcy process from start to finish. In hindsight, I let things get too far out of hand before taking any action. By the time I faced up to reality the one avenue I had not even dared think about had suddenly become my only option.

In the lead up to Christmas 2006, my spiralling debts had got completely out of my control and I finally sought some expert help. The insolvency practitioner who had kindly spared his time free of charge offered me probably the soundest advice I have ever been given, even though it was the last thing I wanted to hear.

Bankruptcy was the one solution I had secretly dreaded. At 32, I was about to lose everything, including my home and job – I was dazed. I experienced a range of emotions, though not all negative. For a while I was filled with varying degrees of anxiety, fear and trepidation. I also felt a fighting spirit burning inside of me.

As I drove home from the meeting I was close to becoming an emotional wreck, my head spinning with endless questions that I could find no answers to. But beneath all of that I was deeply grateful that I had finally been set upon the right path. For the first time in many months I could see a flickering light at the end of a long, dark tunnel.

The seemingly infinite amount of unanswerable questions eventually gave birth to the idea that became this book. The wealth of information and advice I required was spread far and wide across a vast range of agencies and sources. How less fearful I would have felt having had access to the information contained within these pages during those uncertain days.

It is my intention in writing this book to share facts, experiences and possible solutions that others now in a similar situation may be searching for. I have included several of my own personal experiences and perspectives to help shed some light on what might lie ahead for you.

This book describes the complete bankruptcy process from beginning to end, as well as detailing the alternatives to bankruptcy and looking at the independent agencies available to help and advise on the most appropriate solution for you.

In addition, there are sections on how bankruptcy can impact your debts, assets, employment and income. As financial hardship has a significant impact on both the individual and their family, I have included a guide to maintaining a positive outlook, which I hope will provide personal support and encouragement if you require it.

Within just twelve months of the date of your bankruptcy order you should find yourself discharged and quite probably debt-free. Therefore, as well as steps for repairing your credit, I have included advice on budgeting and lifestyle changes which you may find useful in helping you get the most out of your new start.

It should be noted that this book covers the effects of personal insolvency on individuals in England and Wales only. My over-riding intention is to put the appropriate and relevant information into the hands of the people who need it most.

Lee Betteridge, June 2009

How to Survive
Personal Bankruptcy

in England & Wales

Part I: Is Bankruptcy Your Best Option?

1: The Historical Context

The word *bankruptcy* originated from an Italian phrase of medieval times, *banca rotta*, and was used to describe the breaking up of a trader's business due to his failure to pay creditors. In those days Italian moneylenders at market used a bench on which to conduct their business. *Banca*, the Latin word for bench, is where the English word *bank* originates from, *rotta* (in Italian) meaning 'to break'. Therefore, when a moneylender's business failed he was literally required to break up his bench, or see his creditors do it for him!

In the 7th century BC the Greek punishment for bankruptcy was death. However, if lucky, the bankrupt might instead face being sold off into slavery along with the rest of his family, with the proceeds going to repay his creditors.

Some 200 years later the Romans were equally unforgiving. Time, and punishments, had moved on. The price of financial failure was now a maiming, with the creditor being given his pound of flesh in place of the money he could not recover. In the most serious cases the debtor was cut up, with his body parts being distributed amongst his creditors.

By the 13th century Henry III, King of England, had established the practice of throwing debtors into dungeons. Three hundred years later Henry VIII passed the first bankruptcy law which, mercifully, provided remedies other than death, imprisonment or mutilation.

Society was a last coming around to the fact that killing, maiming or locking up debtors was a no-win situation. Creditors would never receive any of their money and the debtor, if lucky enough to survive, never had a chance to make a positive contribution to society.

History does however show evidence of more civilized approaches to the bankruptcy problem. In the 18th century BC the Babylonians passed a law with modern-day echoes, which ordered the bankrupt's possessions to be divided amongst his creditors in proportion to the amount of money owed to each.

The forgiveness of debt has also always been a feature of biblical laws. In Deuteronomy 15: 1-2 it is stated: 'at the end of every seven years, you are to cancel the debts of those who owe you money ... the Lord himself has declared the debt cancelled.' The Israelites of 13th century BC demonstrated a similar approach through the Torah. This provided that every 50th year (Jubilee year) debts were cancelled and slaves were freed.

Generally throughout the ages bankrupts have incurred some terrible penalties which make modern day hardships look like a walk in the park. Fortunately society has taken significant steps forward and today, whilst it cannot be considered an easy option, the process of bankruptcy is thankfully far from life-threatening.

2: Myths

The protection that bankruptcy affords can be a wonderful thing for those to whom it is suited, but all too often the people who would benefit the most from it reject the idea, largely due to fears caused by lack of knowledge of the facts. There are several myths perpetuated about bankruptcy, many of which are exaggerated by unscrupulous companies looking to make money out of vulnerable individuals. Such organisations have been known to actively dissuade clients from bankruptcy in favour of a solution which is of greater benefit to their company's profits, rather than one which is the most suitable for the individual's particular circumstances. These are some of the common bankruptcy myths:

'You will get criminal record and could go to prison'

Bankruptcy is not a criminal offence and you will not go to prison for filing bankruptcy. Where serious fraud is involved this can lead to criminal bankruptcy but such cases are very rare.

If you are deemed to be in some way to blame for your bankruptcy (e.g. you behaved recklessly in borrowing money that you had no means to repay), you might be subject to a court order which extends the restrictions of your bankruptcy for a period of anything from two to fifteen years. And if you were to break such an order you *would* then commit a criminal offence, leaving yourself open to the possibility of a custodial sentence.

'You will lose everything including your home and car'

Although becoming bankrupt will mean that any assets of value will be sold off to repay your creditors, it is far from true to say that you will lose everything. Bankruptcy provides protection, allowing an individual the opportunity to make a fresh start.

What you will keep and what you will lose depends completely on your own particular situation, based on factors such as how much debt you have, the value of your car, whether there is any equity in your home, etc.

The fact is that bankruptcy is a perfectly legal mechanism used to allow you to get back on your feet. You will generally be allowed to keep your household goods, tools required for your trade, and sufficient amount of income to live on. You may also be able to keep your car where you can prove it is a necessity, and maybe even your house, dependent on your own circumstances.

'You will lose your job'

You are not obliged to inform an employer of your bankruptcy unless it is required by your contract of employment. In most instances it is very unlikely that you will lose your job. However, certain positions have bankruptcy restrictions, e.g. jobs involving a degree of financial responsibility. Therefore it is advisable to seek clarification from your employment contract, trade union (if applicable), or Human Resources department regarding any possible effect that bankruptcy may have (see also Chapter 26).

'You cannot have a bank account'

An undischarged bankrupt can apply for a basic bank account, which provides many of the features of a regular current account. You can have your income paid in directly, set up standing orders and direct debits, and use a Visa Electron card for making payments on the high street or on-line. Several financial institutions offer this type of account (see Chapter 13 for further details).

'Bankruptcy makes future credit impossible'

As a bankruptcy will remain on your credit file for a period of six years it is going to take time for you to rebuild your credit rating, but that does not mean that you will find it impossible. It is obviously important that you conduct your finances responsibly after you have been made bankrupt.

Many lenders and finance companies specialise in providing facilities to discharged bankrupts, thus allowing the opportunity to help rebuild their credit profile. As you apply for further accounts or credit, prospective lenders will check your credit performance record and decide on a case-by-case basis whether or not you meet their lending criteria. Eventually there should be no reason why you are not able to apply for loans, credit cards and mortgages.

'You will be publicly humiliated'

The purpose of bankruptcy is not to humiliate, it is to free you from overwhelming debt so that you can turn things around and begin to contribute fully to society once again.

It is true that your bankruptcy is advertised in the London Gazette and in a local newspaper, but this is a necessary part of the process to ensure that any creditors who may have a claim on your bankruptcy estate are made aware of your insolvency.

It is far from a public shaming, and the global credit crunch means that many thousands more will now take advantage of the fresh start that bankruptcy offers in order to get their lives back on track.

3: The Process and the Players

Overview of the process

A bankruptcy order is only made by a court where a petition has been presented. A debtor's petition is heard when the individual concerned initiates proceedings. A creditor's petition is brought by one or more creditors who are owed at least £750 unsecured debt.

It is important that you co-operate fully once bankruptcy proceedings have begun, whether you agree with the petition or not. Refusing to acknowledge the proceedings will not prevent a bankruptcy order being made.

Upon discharge from bankruptcy, which usually occurs after a maximum of twelve months, you will become free from most debts.

The players

There are three main officials that will deal directly with your bankruptcy – the *court judge*, the *Official Receiver*, and an *insolvency practitioner* who may be appointed to act as trustee. The Official Receiver (an officer of the court) will be appointed to deal with your bankruptcy, and in turn he or she may appoint an insolvency practitioner to act as trustee of your estate.

The judge has a crucial role in the process, as it is he or she who will decide whether granting a bankruptcy order is appropriate based on the circumstances of your case (see Chapter 16).

The Official Receiver is a civil servant and an officer of the court and is responsible for protecting your assets from the date of the bankruptcy order.

If you have no assets, the Official Receiver will also act as your trustee in bankruptcy.

It is the Official Receiver who will investigate your financial affairs for the period before and during your bankruptcy, having a duty to report any matters which indicate that you may have committed criminal offences in relation to your bankruptcy. The Official Receiver will also establish whether your behaviour has been dishonest or you have been in some way to blame for your bankruptcy.

In addition your Official Receiver will also give notice of the bankruptcy to other relevant bodies, e.g. other courts, HM Revenue and Customs and the Land Registry. In investigating the details of assets or liabilities you have, the Official Receiver will also make enquiries of financial institutions, solicitors and landlords etc.

An insolvency practitioner is appointed if you have significant assets and acts as your trustee in bankruptcy. An insolvency practitioner is a licensed individual who specialises in bankruptcy work. Once an order has been made against you, your creditors can no longer pursue you for payment. The trustee takes on the responsibility to dispose of your assets and make payments to your creditors.

4: The Insolvency Service

The Insolvency Service deal with insolvency matters in England and Wales. The service operates under the Insolvency Acts of 1986 and 2000 and includes a network of Official Receiver offices.

The service undertakes a wide range of activities including, but not limited to:

• administering and investigating the affairs of bankrupts, companies and partnerships to establish the reasons behind the insolvency

• acting as trustee when no insolvency practitioner is appointed

• acting as nominee/supervisor in *individual voluntary arrangements* (IVA), an alternative to bankruptcy (see Chapter 6)

• taking forward reports of bankrupts' misconduct

• dealing with restrictions placed upon the bankrupt

• authorising and regulating the insolvency profession

• providing information to the public on insolvency and redundancy matters via the internet, leaflets and the Insolvency Enquiry Line telephone service

The Insolvency Service website contains a wide range of information on insolvency legislation, including the contact details of Official Receivers' offices and answers to the most frequently asked questions. Further information is available at **www.insolvency.gov.uk**. It should be noted that neither the Insolvency Service nor Official Receivers can give legal or financial advice regarding the most appropriate solution.

Complete your bankruptcy petition online

There are several services available via the Insolvency Service website, one of the most useful being the ability to complete your bankruptcy forms online. The forms, which you must complete in order to make yourself bankrupt, are the *petition* and the *statement of affairs*.

Finding an insolvency practitioner or Official Receiver

The online menu provides links to searchable databases containing contact details of licensed insolvency practitioners and Official Receivers in England and Wales.

Insolvency Enquiry Line

This service provides general information on insolvency legislation and procedures, including the work of Official Receivers' offices. The telephone number is 0845 602 9848 and is available Monday to Friday from 9am to 5pm.

5: Pros and Cons

Bankruptcy has many potential consequences, both positive and negative, dependent on your own circumstances. A brief overview of the major effects is given below, with further details provided in the pages that follow.

Advantages

- Bankruptcy frees you from overwhelming debt so you can make a fresh start.
- Creditors deal directly with your trustee in bankruptcy, eliminating harassment and significantly reducing stress.
- Under the Insolvency Act 1986, you are allowed to keep certain possessions including household goods, the tools of your trade, and even your car if you can prove that it is a necessity.
- Following the Enterprise Act 2002, an individual is normally automatically discharged from bankruptcy after twelve months, or sooner if the Official Receiver completes his investigations early.

Disadvantages

- It costs money to become bankrupt (currently £495).
- Your home may be sold to release funds towards payment of your debt, in addition to your car and any other valuable assets.
- Your bankruptcy is advertised in The London Gazette, an official publication which contains legal notices, and in a local or national newspaper (possibly both).
- You may be required to make contributions towards your bankruptcy debts for a period of three years under an income payments order (see Chapter 27).

- Secured debts are not included in a bankruptcy. Additionally, certain debts are not written off, e.g. student loans, court fines and child maintenance payments.
- If you own a business it is likely to be closed down, with your employees being dismissed and any assets sold off.
- You will be subject to certain restrictions during the term of your bankruptcy, e.g. having to declare your status if applying for credit of £500 or more, being unable to act as a company director.
- If you are deemed to be in some way to blame for your bankruptcy, you could be subjected to a bankruptcy restrictions order or undertaking (see Chapter 18) which can extend the restrictions for a period anywhere between two and fifteen years.
- Bankruptcies are registered with credit reference agencies and will stay on your credit file for a minimum of six years.
- If you are a member of a professional body bankruptcy may result in the loss of your membership, which could mean you are unable to continue in your current role.
- Where you have joint debts, creditors can pursue the other party for the full outstanding amount.
- You may lose any assets obtained during your bankruptcy, e.g. an inheritance received from a will.
- You must co-operate fully in the scrutinising of your financial affairs by the Official Receiver and trustee, and you may have to go to court to explain why you are in debt.

6: Your Alternatives

When you are considering bankruptcy it is imperative that you weigh up all of your options. The consequences can be very serious.

There are several formal and informal options available to you that may prevent the need for bankruptcy. The option or combination of options that are right for you will depend wholly on your current circumstances, including your employment status, your family situation, and the property and assets you hold, amongst many others.

There are lifestyle changes you can make to tighten your belt and help you ride out the storm. You can explore the opportunity of releasing equity held in your property, or sell your car and buy a cheaper alternative. Maybe you could take a second or part-time job to increase your income, or use cheaper outlets to purchase food and clothes. Discontinuing the use of any credit cards will also help.

This chapter takes a look at the possible alternatives to bankruptcy. Once you are aware of the available options you should talk through your situation in detail with an appropriate professional adviser before deciding.

The main alternatives to bankruptcy are:

- Administration Order
- Informal Arrangement (e.g. Debt Management Plan)
- Individual Voluntary Arrangement (IVA)
- Debt Relief Order (implemented April 2009)

1. Administration Order

An administration order is a court order that deals with the total sum you owe to your creditors. Under the order an individual makes a single affordable payment every month into the court. The court then distributes the money on a pro-rata basis amongst the creditors.

No creditor included in the order is able to take any action against you without permission of the court. Interest and other charges being added to the debts are stopped. Visits from debt collectors, letters or phone calls from your creditors will also cease as a result of the order.

Process

The court will make an order based on what you can afford. You must have enough regular income to make a weekly or monthly payment. The order states how much you will pay and for how long.

The court will often require you to continue payments until your debts are cleared in full, although some orders only require a percentage to be repaid. The order may also state that the amount you repay each week or month will be reviewed from time to time.

There is no up-front fee to pay to the court for an administration order. The court will take a handling fee of 10 percent out of every £1 you pay for the time the order lasts.

Criteria

To be eligible to apply for an administration order you must fulfil the following criteria: your total debt must not exceed £5,000; you must have at least one county court or High Court judgement against you, and you must have a minimum of two creditors. You can apply for an administration order by completing Form N92 which is available from your local court office.

Failure to keep up with payments

If you fail to keep up with the payments the court can cancel the administration order. This enables your creditors to take action against you towards recovering the outstanding amounts owed to them. Therefore it is imperative that you ask the court to review the order and reduce the payments if you find that you are no longer able to afford them.

Administration orders and your credit rating

Administration orders are recorded in the Register of County Court Judgments, and this could make it difficult for you to obtain credit in the future. After paying the administration order off you can get a Certificate of Satisfaction from the county court for a fee of fifteen pounds.

Details of your administration order are also kept by the credit reference agencies. On application the agencies should amend your file to show the debts and the administration order have been satisfied.

2. Informal Arrangement

An informal arrangement might also be referred to as a 'family arrangement' or a 'debt management plan'. If you are unable to make payments on time, you may consider writing to each of your creditors to agree a compromise. Your proposal should consist of a timetable setting out a plan detailing when you will make repayments.

Is an informal arrangement right for you?

Such arrangements are suitable where there is little money available to repay your debts, or where you are currently having problems making your payments but are likely to be able to make the normal repayments again within a few months. An informal arrangement may also be a solution in circumstances where you cannot afford the full monthly repayment but you can afford a regular amount each month.

Initially you need to work out how much you can afford to repay your creditors each month after you have paid your essential living expenses. You then write to each creditor explaining the situation and requesting that they accept the lower payment until your situation improves and you can make the full repayments.

Advantages of an informal arrangement

The main advantage is that it can be set up by you or your adviser quickly and is free. In addition, it offers an effective solution if your problem is short term and your creditors accept lower payments.

Disadvantages of an informal arrangement

The main obstacle is convincing your creditors to accept reduced payments, as they are under no obligation to do so. Even if they accept, they are free to change their minds at any time. They may only be willing to accept the arrangement as a short term measure.

Debt Management Plan (DMP)

One specific type of informal arrangement is a debt management plan. These agreements are usually brokered by companies who negotiate with creditors on your behalf. Your monthly payment is calculated at an amount you can afford and you pay this directly to the debt management company. The company, in turn, make the payment to the administrator of the plan, who then distributes the money to your creditors in amounts proportionate to the amount owed to each one.

Advantages of a DMP

- Monthly commitments can be met with a single payment
- The plan allows you to free up monthly income so that you can live more comfortably

- Your interest payments may be frozen and your repayment term extended
- You are spared the time and hassle of negotiating directly with your creditors

Disadvantages of a DMP

- A DMP is not legally binding, so creditors are free to proceed with court action against you.
- Debt management companies will usually only take on customers who have available income and own their own home, enabling the home to be used as surety against the debts.
- Many debt management companies will not deal with priority debts (where certain creditors have first call on any payments). You will have to deal with such debts yourself.
- Some debt management companies charge a substantial fee, typically £200, leaving you less money to distribute to your creditors. The majority of companies also charge a monthly administration fee to cover the cost of distribution of payments to creditors, sometimes around £30 per month.
- Many debt management companies do not offer financial advice, meaning that the customer will not be given details of other possible options open to them.
- If your monthly payment is low and your debts are high, it could take you many years to clear your debt.

3. Individual Voluntary Arrangement (IVA)

An IVA is a formal arrangement, generally appropriate for people who have some money available to pay their creditors each month but cannot meet the monthly repayment in full. Should the creditors agree to an IVA, it can mean that some of the debt may be written off. The IVA is a legally binding agreement on both you and your creditors. If you break the terms of the IVA you could be made bankrupt.

Who is it suitable for?

There is no maximum or minimum level of debt and no maximum or minimum level of repayments, other than what is acceptable to your creditors. An IVA may be suitable if you have enough disposable income to make regular payments, or you have relatives or friends prepared to help contribute towards your debts.

How it works

To set up an IVA you will need the services of a licensed insolvency practitioner. Contact details of local insolvency practitioners are available from your Official Receiver's office, and can also be found online through the Association of Business Recovery Professionals (known as R3) at www.r3.org.uk, or via the Insolvency Service website at www.insolvency.gov.uk. The majority of insolvency practitioners are accountants or solicitors, and it would be advisable to contact several to find out what they charge before asking one to act.

The insolvency practitioner (who becomes your nominee) will draft a formal proposal to your creditors to pay part or all of your debts. This is based on a full breakdown of your current financial situation, including assets held, such as a share in a property. He will also calculate your essential living expenses, deducting the figure from your income to provide the amount of your disposable income.

It will also set out how much you intend to pay into the IVA and include details of any other assets included in the funds that you are able to draw on.

Once prepared, your nominee will assess the proposal and gauge whether it has a reasonable chance of being agreed with the creditors. If so, a meeting of creditors will be arranged to present it. Here the creditors will vote on whether to accept your proposals. Creditors holding over 75 percent of the total debt must vote in favour in order for the proposal to be accepted. On approval, the agreement binds every creditor who received or was entitled to receive notice of the meeting. Your nominee will be appointed to supervise the IVA and pay the creditors in accordance with the accepted proposal.

Advantages of an IVA over bankruptcy

An IVA will give you more say in how your assets are dealt with and how payments are made to your creditors. By acting responsibly and with flexibility in the dealings with your creditors, you may be able to persuade them to allow you to keep certain assets, e.g. your home. You will also avoid the restrictions that are placed on a bankrupt.

What is the duration of an IVA?

An IVA will generally last five years, but this may vary depending on the details of your proposal. It ends when all sums set out in the proposal are paid. Where you are unable to keep to the terms of the arrangement it will fail, which could then lead to bankruptcy.

If an IVA is agreed, the details of it are entered on the Individual Insolvency Register (an online register maintained by the Insolvency Service) which may affect your ability to obtain credit.

4. Debt Relief Order (DRO)

Debt relief orders came into effect in April 2009, and provide a non court-based scheme for people with low debts, little surplus income and few assets, who cannot pay off their debts in a reasonable time. The order will lead to the debts being discharged after twelve months if the debtor's circumstances have not changed.

The criteria to apply a debt relief order (DRO)

To qualify for a debt relief order, the following conditions must be met:

- the debtor is unable to pay his or her debts
- total unsecured liabilities do not exceed £15,000
- total gross assets do not exceed £300 (although you may own a car to the value of £1000)
- total disposable income, following deduction of normal household expenses, does not exceed £50 per month
- the debtor is domiciled in England or Wales, or in the last three years has been resident or carried on business in England or Wales
- the debtor has not previously been subject to a DRO within the last six years
- the debtor is not involved in another formal insolvency procedure at the time of application for a DRO, e.g. bankruptcy or IVA

Application process

A DRO is obtained by seeking advice from a debt adviser. If a DRO appears to be appropriate an approved intermediary will help to complete the application. An intermediary is a trained debt adviser who has been approved to act as an intermediary by a competent authority.

The intermediary will complete basic checks on the information provided by the debtor, e.g. by considering paperwork and evidence of income and debts. Where it is considered that a DRO is suitable in the circumstances detailed by a debtor, the intermediary will help to complete the application upon the debtor's request.

On receipt of the application and associated fee an Official Receiver can make the order administratively, without the involvement of the court, if it appears that the applicant meets the requirements.

The Official Receiver can refuse to make on order, or can delay the decision pending the receipt of further information from the applicant.

The fee for a DRO is currently £90.

Effects of a DRO

Whilst the order is in force the debtor will be:

- protected from enforcement action by creditors included in the application (except in the case of certain creditors whose debts cannot be scheduled into the DRO, and also any creditors whose debts are included but have successfully obtained leave from the court to pursue them).
- free from those debts at the end of the period (usually twelve months).
- obliged to co-operate with the Official Receiver and provide requested information.
- expected to make arrangements to repay their creditors if their financial circumstances improve.

The debtor's credit rating will be affected by the DRO. Additionally, the Official Receiver is able to undertake investigations, either on his or her own account or as the result of an objection by creditors. The order can be revoked if the debtor is found to have failed to provide a full and accurate account of their financial affairs, e.g. understatement of assets or income. Civil and criminal penalties may be applied to those who abuse the system.

Restrictions

For the duration of the order the debtor will be subject to similar restrictions as in bankruptcy and their details will be held on the publically-available Individual Insolvency Register. Under the restrictions the debtor:

- must not obtain credit of £500 or more, either solely or jointly, without informing the lender that they are subject to a DRO.
- may not carry on a business, either directly or indirectly, in a name that is different from the name under which they were granted a DRO, without telling all they do business with the name under which they were granted a DRO.

- without permission of the court, may not be involved, either directly or indirectly, with the promotion, management or formation of a limited company, and may not act as a company director.
- can only obtain a DRO once in any six-year period.

The Official Receiver will be able to apply for a debt relief restrictions order, similar to a bankruptcy restrictions order, which can extend the restriction period for up to fifteen years for debtors who are found to be dishonest or culpable.

7: Living Abroad?

If you are currently living abroad, there are different rules governing your ability to file for bankruptcy in England and Wales, depending on which country you are in. One set of regulations governs EU member states (excluding Denmark), with separate laws applicable to Denmark and elsewhere in the world.

European Union Member States (excluding Denmark)

If you are living in a European Union member state, except Denmark, a bankruptcy order made in England and Wales will be accepted in all EU countries, which means that debts in all EU countries will be administered under the single order and the rules that apply in that country. However, under the EC Regulation on Insolvency Proceedings you can only make yourself bankrupt in the country where you have your 'centre of main interest' (COMI).

The centre of main interest is not specifically defined, but the court will usually regard the country where you earn your living or carry on a business as your centre of main interest. Additionally the court will also take into account the place where you normally reside, i.e. your country of habitual residence.

If you are not in any type of employment your centre of main interest will be the country you normally live in at the date of your petition. Consequently, in this case, if you do not live or work in England and Wales you cannot petition for bankruptcy there.

The rest of the world, including Denmark

If you reside in Denmark or another part of the world you can petition for bankruptcy in England and Wales, provided you are personally present in the UK on the day you make your petition to the court or if you have lived or carried on business in England and Wales in the previous three years.

However, the country in which you reside may not recognise the bankruptcy proceedings. As a result creditors may still be able to take action against you in the country concerned.

Note: Northern Ireland and Scotland have different rules to the rest of the UK (which comply with overall EU law as described above). If your centre of main interest is in either country, then you must apply for bankruptcy under the appropriate jurisdiction.

If you are unsure whether you qualify to file for bankruptcy in England and Wales you should call the Insolvency Service Enquiry Line on 0845 602 9848 to obtain further guidance.

8: Get Independent Professional Advice

Whether bankruptcy is the ideal solution for you will depend on a range of factors, including the specifics of your debts, income, assets, family and employment. But taking professional advice is paramount. Not only is it good sense, but also a prerequisite of the bankruptcy process, and if overlooked could mean that your petition is dismissed.

Often a person can be too closely involved in a situation to have a balanced perspective. Having an extra pair of eyes assess your situation could save you a lot of heartache in the future. What you currently believe to be the right option may actually not serve you very well. There is a lot at stake, and making the correct decision could be the difference between beginning a new stress-free life and struggling under a huge financial strain indefinitely.

You may be of the opinion that there isn't really much of a problem and you can work things out on your own. That may well prove to be the case, but I would strongly urge anyone who has been compelled to seek out the information contained in these pages to get an impartial view from an independent professional adviser.

You have no need to have concerns about laying your cards on the table before a complete stranger. By choosing an established independent advice agency you can be assured that you will not be judged. There is a saying that *bad debt happens to good people*, and it is truer today than ever before.

Several major professional debt advice agencies are mentioned in the following pages to indicate the range of help available. Many of the agencies offer their services free of charge. You can take advice from one or several, or indeed seek out your own preferred options.

Whilst I would urge you to seek help you should also take some care in choosing it. There are unscrupulous companies out there who will be only too happy to help you – help you to help them make money. So take advice, but don't at any point feel pressured into anything. Trust your gut feeling, and if in doubt – walk away.

Advice agencies

The following organisations will provide you with a good starting point on your road to financial freedom:

- **Citizens Advice**

Citizens Advice and each Citizens Advice Bureau (CAB) are registered charities based in local communities. They provide free, confidential and independent advice from over 3,200 locations within the UK. Advice is available face-to-face and by telephone, with many offices offering home visits and e-mail support. CAB help people resolve a multitude of problems including debt, benefits, housing, legal and employment issues. Their services are available to everybody regardless of race, nationality or religion.

- **Adviceguide**

Adviceguide is the Citizens Advice online service that provides independent advice on your rights. Adviceguide can be found at www.adviceguide.org.uk and offers practical, up-to-date information on a wide range of topics. The information can be accessed in several different languages, with a large number of fact sheets available for download directly from the website.

The site is arranged into helpful sections: 'Your money' deals with debt, benefits, employment and tax issues; 'Your family' gives advice on a huge spectrum of family matters including issues involving health, housing and education; 'Your daily life' deals with communications, consumer affairs and travel; 'Your rights' covers the areas of discrimination, civil rights, immigration and aspects of the legal system.

Their online search facility will provide you with the contact details of the Citizens Advice office local to you. CAB operates out of diverse locations including GP surgeries, hospitals, colleges, prisons and courts and is readily accessible throughout the UK.

- **Consumer Credit Counselling Service (CCCS)**

The Consumer Credit Counselling Service is a registered charity providing free confidential advice and support for debt problems. The service ranges from immediate debt advice tailored to individual circumstances or more general budgeting advice. The CCCS provides a free national telephone advice service, ten regional centres and an online CCCS Debt Remedy, which can be accessed at www.cccs.co.uk.

Online, Debt Remedy gathers information specific to your own circumstances. It takes around 20 minutes to complete the process, after which you will receive a CCCS Debt Remedy tailored to your own personal situation. You remain anonymous and the service is free. Their approach is based on a proven and successful formula. The service provides counselling on personal budgeting; advice on the use of credit, and setting up achievable repayment plans.

Should you prefer to telephone rather than using the online remedy, the Freephone helpline number is 0800 138 1111. An adviser will assess your situation and offer appropriate guidance, such as emergency help, self-help materials, or a counselling appointment.

Whether you complete the online debt remedy or have a counselling appointment, your circumstances will be thoroughly reviewed before you are given a recommendation for the most appropriate way forward. The CCCS may ask your creditors to freeze interest, stop penalties and charges, and accept a longer repayment period and sometimes even a reduced sum.

- **National Debtline**

National Debtline is a telephone helpline that provides free confidential and independent advice on how to deal with debt problems. The service provides self-help advice to its callers and can assist with the setting up of debt management plans free of charge.

When you call, a trained adviser will gather information from you about your personal financial situation before outlining the options available, along with the pros and cons of each. The advisers are non-judgmental and treat all calls in the strictest confidence. You can remain anonymous if you wish; there is no obligation to divulge any personal details.

Their website address is www.nationaldebtline.co.uk. Using the site you can download a debt information pack and work out what level of repayments are affordable using the personal budget section. Sample letters are available for use when writing to creditors and various factsheets are available. Advisors can be contacted on 0808 808 4000 and advice is also available via e-mail.

- **Payplan**

Payplan provide free debt advice and solutions for anyone experiencing financial difficulties. Their service is impartial and non-judgemental. Payplan provide debt solutions including free debt management plans and IVA's, and their experienced debt advisors can be contacted on 0800 917 7823 or www.payplan.com.

- **Insolvency practitioner**

Licensed insolvency practitioners can provide expert advice on specific debt solutions such as bankruptcy and individual voluntary arrangements. As legislation and case law are regularly being amended, insolvency practitioners are best placed to advise on how you will be affected. Many will provide an initial consultation free of charge and without obligation.

I myself was fortunate enough to be offered a free 60-minute consultation, an hour which turned out to be one of the most beneficial of my life.

Practitioners can be found via the Insolvency Service website or by using the Association of Business Recovery Professionals (R3) site at www.r3.org.uk.

- **Solicitor**

Any specific legal advice you require is best sought from a solicitor. Of course, legal advice can be expensive so it is worth shopping around. Decide on what sort of solicitor you need to speak to and get quotes from several. Many solicitors charge little or nothing for a short first interview. To find solicitors in your area, you can consult the website www.lawsociety.org.uk.

- **Shelter (for housing debt advice)**

Shelter is a charity that provides confidential help to people with all types of housing problems, e.g. mortgage problems; if your landlord is facing an order for repossession on the property you are living in, or if you require housing immediately.

The charity can be contacted on 0808 800 4444. Calls are free from UK landlines, and their trained housing advisers are available seven days a week. They can offer immediate practical assistance, explain your rights, offer advice and guidance, and suggest specialist or local support services to help you long term.

The charity has more than fifty offices across Britain. You can write for advice, and some centres also have drop-in sessions. Many of the centres also have surgeries in areas away from their office. Advice can also be obtained by email using the website at www.shelter.org.uk. Although Shelter does not operate in Wales it is affiliated to a housing charity with a similar mission – Shelter Cymru. The website address for Shelter Cymru is www.sheltercymru.org.uk.

- **Online debt forums**

Forums can be a useful source of information and support where members share experiences regarding a whole range of debt problems. However, very few are regulated by legal professionals and so any information given, whilst well intended, may not be accurate. Always seek clarification from a competent professional adviser before taking any action.

Part II: Turning Your Life Around

9: Changing Your Thinking

If you get up one more time than you fall you will make it through
– Chinese proverb

When faced with difficult financial circumstances it is all too easy to begin beating yourself up. You may feel that you could have made other choices, or come to different decisions that would have avoided the tough situation you now find yourself in. While you may have made mistakes along the way, nothing positive will be gained by making yourself suffer through feelings of guilt.

You are where you are. Make peace with that and try to resist the temptation of looking back to pinpoint what went wrong and when. You can never find a solution whilst focussing on a problem. Giving your attention to the things that have gone wrong in the past will hold back your progress in putting things right now and in the future.

So the first step is to give yourself a break and stop feeling bad. I realise this is easier said than done but with a little practice you will begin to feel better and better, and before you know it your problems will begin to appear insignificant in the light of the bright debt-free future you can now expect.

The following pages address some common negative thoughts along with suggestions on how you might deal with them.

I feel like such a failure; how was I so stupid?

Okay, so things didn't work out as planned. Your inner critic has probably had a field day, raining blow after blow on your already battered self-esteem. 'How could you be so stupid? What were you thinking? You thought you were so clever. You should have known. They told you it wouldn't work out.' Okay, got that out of your system? Now it's time to stop beating yourself up.

From the beginning your intentions were positive. Maybe you were looking to improve some aspect of your life, be that by purchasing a new house; by taking a well-earned holiday abroad; or demonstrating your faith in a friend by backing their business vision. Then somewhere along the line the plan became derailed. Perhaps you didn't fully consider all of the potential pitfalls. It happens. Make peace with it. Take action to address the situation, and then let it go and move on with your life.

Hindsight is always a wonderful thing. Of course life would be much easier if we could preview the end result before we made major decisions. Getting one decision wrong doesn't make you inferior or lacking in intelligence. Instead you should feel proud that you had the courage to take a chance, to back your vision and go for it.

Every single successful person has had far more failures than successes. You are always going to make mistakes in life, that fact is unavoidable. But instead of beating yourself up and going into hiding to lick your wounds, lift your head up and show the world how resilient you are. Through the experience you have gained invaluable knowledge that will benefit you greatly as you make decisions in the future. There really is no substitute for experience.

Aiming to achieve anything worthwhile in life always comes with some element of risk, and mistakes always have consequences. Fortunately, suffering financial pain can be nothing more than a temporary glitch in your life.

Take the positives from the situation. Be thankful for an experience through which you have learned so much. Celebrate the fact that you are a survivor – I do that now, and so will you.

I feel ashamed; people will think I'm a loser

One thing you need to get clear in your mind is that you have absolutely nothing to feel shame for. Very few people borrow money without intending to pay it back. Life has a habit of throwing unwelcome problems in the way: the car exhaust begins blowing; an unexpected tax bill arrives; fuel prices increase yet again; the central heating boiler breaks down ....

No matter how carefully you plan and budget, the impact caused by an unexpected bill can destroy the best laid financial plans like a tornado. So you borrowed money that you were ultimately unable to repay? – get over it. You are not a criminal and will not be treated like one. Feeling guilty will only serve to undermine your efforts to put the situation right. Thousands of people are currently becoming bankrupt each and every month, and everyone deserves and receives a fresh start. Take it, embrace it, and move forward.

Another common destructive feeling that serves no useful purpose is that of trying to second-guess what other people will make of your circumstances. The belief that other people will gain any kind of satisfaction from your predicament is a long way wide of the mark. You will more likely discover that others will want to give you encouragement and support.

Since the time I myself experienced these feelings, I have realised that what other people may or may not think is none of my business anyway. The most empowering moment for me was the realisation of the fact I could truly rely on myself one hundred percent. I gained strength, focus and resilience, which helped me regain complete control of my life.

I feel worn out

The constant stress and worry brought about by living life under a financial cloud can have a very real physical impact. Sleepless nights can become a normal occurrence, leading to an almost constant feeling of tiredness and exhaustion, in turn leading to lethargy throughout the day. By the time night comes around the recurring worry and inability to get a restful sleep perpetuates a vicious cycle.

I have always enjoyed driving and the sense of freedom it allowed me, being able to jump in the car and within minutes be miles away, taking in completely contrasting sights and surroundings. My old BMW did not make it as far as my bankruptcy, the engine blew up on the west-bound section of the M62 north of Manchester a few months before – an omen of things to come, perhaps? But my urge to wander didn't cease with my lack of wheels. I found it to be a great therapy to get out of the house and walk – anywhere – for miles! Walking, no matter what the weather, helped me think and provided a welcome distraction, helping to put my mind at ease. At such times I was untouchable, unable to be harassed by the sound of the telephone, or by debt collectors turning up unexpectedly at the house.

Research has proven that a great way for people to combat depression is to get out of the house and walk around the neighbourhood. Escaping the four walls has been shown to be of great benefit. Whilst I was not depressed, I did feel a great relief by getting out into the fresh air. In tiring myself out walking I also had the added benefit of being assisted in sleeping better at night. Therefore I would feel less tired the next day, and more likely to get out of bed and face the world again.

I'm scared of the process

Although at first glance the bankruptcy process can seem daunting and overwhelming, by focusing on each task in turn you will soon make real progress and gain a great deal of self-confidence. Within the pages of this book you have a step-by-step guide to help you through the entire process so you will know exactly what to expect.

Many of the scaremongering stories about bankruptcy are far from true. Try not to worry – the journey is far less scary that you have probably imagined. Perhaps you are about to undertake your Official Receiver interview, or maybe you have still not made the decision on whether bankruptcy is the correct solution for you. No matter what stage you are at, the most practical approach is to focus on dealing only with the very next step.

By successfully negotiating each obstacle, you will gradually clear a way through the insolvency jungle. Deal with the process chunk by chunk, and like tackling an obstacle course, the further you progress the stronger and more confident you will become.

When dealing with the various professionals who will administer your case, remember that they have a job to do. They are not there to judge or condemn you, merely to assist in dealing with your bankruptcy. It is very unlikely that you will meet discourtesy. The officials have been through the process on countless previous occasions, and for the most part you are likely to find them helpful and understanding.

Should you be worried about getting through the day of your bankruptcy hearing it may be of benefit for you to take a friend along to the court for support. As there can be a lot of sitting around and waiting you may prefer to have your mind occupied. It is of course down to individual preference; personally I wanted to deal with the hearing alone. Just take whatever steps will make you feel most comfortable.

I don't think I can cope

'If you fall stand tall and come back for more' – Tupac Shakur

No matter what your current circumstances, there are very few problems that cannot be overcome, financially or otherwise. Your health and mental well-being are far more important than any debt issues you may have. Money is just paper, not a matter of life and death. If you find you are struggling to cope then please don't be afraid to contact a professional counsellor for help, you can always do so in the strictest confidence. You are not alone, and it is not necessary for you to attempt to deal with the situation on your own.

In the current economic climate there are many thousands of people enduring sleepless nights as they struggle to hold back the tide. Countless others have become abruptly aware of an overpowering lack of security that just a few years ago seemed unthinkable. But the reality is that you can get through these difficulties, whether you choose bankruptcy or not.

For me, on a personal level, losing everything was a truly empowering experience. It gave me the strength to come out fighting. I became aware of qualities I never knew I possessed. And the support of those close to me was all that I had hoped for and more.

It is very rare that anyone borrows money without intending to repay it. But many people, myself included, made mistakes along the way. Make peace with that – it is life.

Getting through bankruptcy will lead you to discoveries about yourself that you wouldn't otherwise have made, and before too long you will look back at the experience and appreciate it as the catalyst through which you grew stronger and more resilient. Dr Robert H Schuller summed up the situation perfectly: *Tough times never last, but tough people do.* Bankruptcy really can be a blessing in disguise.

I'm scared to tell my partner / family / friends

Bankruptcy provides a fresh start in more ways than one, not only freeing you from the shackles of insurmountable debt, but also in allowing the perfect opportunity to bring any other contributory skeletons out of the closet, e.g. a compulsive spending habit. It is unlikely that anyone is going to judge you, and even if someone does, they are not really the type of person you want to include in your life in any case.

Although personally I could have tried to cover-up my predicament, it was never an option I considered. I wasn't ashamed. I was taking back control of my life, and anyone who was going to hold what had happened against me wasn't going to be part of my life anymore.

I actually began to feel blessed for the situation that I had found myself in. Some people who I had considered good friends were suddenly nowhere to be found. Others, who I viewed as mere acquaintances, were giving genuine support. Bankruptcy was teaching me an unexpected but very welcome lesson.

My bankruptcy meant that resigning from my job at the bank was unavoidable. However, after a period of unemployment, I began a new job at a local hotel and met a whole new crowd of people. The friendships I made there were honest in that those people were around me for who I was, not what I did or didn't have.

So don't worry what the reaction of people around you may be. You are facing up to a difficult set of circumstances and should be applauded for your actions. People will move in and out of your life and alongside the debt that you are casting off you can sweep a broom through other areas of your life too. It really is a case of out with the old and in with the new.

Worry not! The pleasures that await you far outweigh the pain!
'Every negative event contains within it the seed of an equal or greater benefit' – Napoleon Hill

It is true that being under the strain of huge debt can have a major impact on your health and relationships. But it need not be that way. Believe me when I say that any current fears you have are far worse than the reality that will play out.

Research has shown that around ninety percent of future events people worry about never come to pass. Mark Twain, the world renowned author who also survived bankruptcy, put it into to context when he said: 'I have been through some terrible things in my life, some of which actually happened'.

Try and cast aside any fear you may be feeling, it does not serve you and is unnecessary. What you will gain through the experience far outweighs anything you may lose. Possessions are only temporary in any case. You will soon have a solid stable platform from which to get them all back and more.

But far more valuable than any material asset is the feeling of relief you will experience when you are no longer tied to debt which has been weighing like an anchor. Once you cast off the anchor, there are no more unpayable bills, no hassling creditors or bailiffs, and no more sleepless nights.

What you will gain is immeasurable. Nothing is more valuable than your freedom. So take back control of your life. The only regret you will have is that you didn't do it sooner.

10: You Are Not Alone

Record Bankruptcy Figures Announced

Rocketing numbers of consumers fell victim to the financial crisis during 2008, with the Insolvency Service figures revealing that a record number of people in England and Wales were declared bankrupt during the final quarter of the year.

19,100 people were made bankrupt (on a seasonally-adjusted basis) in the three months to the end of December – a 22 percent increase on the same period of 2007. The figure was the highest since records began in 1960, overtaking the record set during the previous quarter, and contributed to a total of 67,428 people being declared bankrupt during the whole of 2008, also a new high.

The total number of people declared insolvent during the year, including those who had entered an IVA, stood at 106,544, equating to 350 people every day. During the three year period ending in December 2008 there were a staggering 320,477 personal insolvencies, of which 194,864 were bankruptcies.

Economists warned that the level of bankruptcies was set to climb further as unemployment rose and the credit crunch meant households could not borrow their way out of trouble. The housing market continued to experience falling house prices and was likely to face further pressure as banks began repossessing debtors' homes. More than 150,000 people were expected to be declared bankrupt, enter into an IVA or a debt relief order during 2009.

Struggling under a mountain of debt can seem an isolating and lonely experience, but as the 2008 figures show, you are certainly not alone in your predicament. Help and solutions are out there, and with many professional services being offered free of charge there really is no need to suffer in silence. So however grave you think your situation might be, make that call, and feel the welcome relief of taking a huge step towards regaining control of your finances and your future.

The Bankrupts Who Became Millionaires

'Success is not final, failure is not fatal: it is the courage to continue that counts.'- Sir Winston Churchill

Throughout history men and women from all manner of backgrounds have tasted the bitter pill of bankruptcy, which only served to fan the flames of their 'never-say-die' attitude. As inspirational statesman and writer Sir Winston Churchill observed: 'Success is the ability to go from failure to failure without loss of enthusiasm.' These are a few of the individuals who were persistent in the face of adversity:

Walt Disney

Walt Disney, the Oscar winning film producer, animator and theme park pioneer, was beset by financial difficulties after starting his first film company Laugh-O-Gram in 1921. Within two years the fledgling company encountered distribution problems. With Walt unable to cover costs, the studio was forced into bankruptcy.

Undeterred, he moved to Hollywood, and began his meteoric rise to fame. The name Walt Disney became huge the world over, with current annual revenue of over $35 billion.

Henry Ford

It is ironic that the Ford Motor Company has flirted with bankruptcy during the recent credit crunch, as the company founder, Henry Ford, had experienced similar problems around a century earlier.

His first venture, the Detroit Automobile Company, was bankrupt within two years. Ford formed another, the Henry Ford Company, but left the group after a disagreement with a business partner.

It was to be a case of third time lucky, however, when he launched the Ford Motor Company in 1903, which is now the world's fourth largest motor vehicle manufacturer.

H J Heinz

At 25, Henry John Heinz started a company producing processed condiments. Several years later, a business panic unexpectedly bankrupted him, driving away friends and business associates.

Within a few short months Heinz had got together with his brother and a cousin to begin a new venture making ketchup. The business was a phenomenal success and today H J Heinz Company boasts annual revenue in excess of $10 billion.

Cyndi Lauper

Grammy-award-winning singer and songwriter Cyndi Lauper suffered some major setbacks before she eventually hit the big-time. At one point she damaged her vocal cords and was informed by doctors that she would never sing again. Unperturbed, she bounced back, joining a band and releasing a debut album. But after a lawsuit was filed against the band by a former manager, Lauper was forced into bankruptcy.

Once again the singer refused to let go of her dream and began singing in local clubs. Eventually she secured a record deal which would lead to the release of 11 albums, selling in excess of 25 million albums and singles worldwide.

Rowland Hussey Macy

Rowland H Macy, Sr was the founder of the Macy department store chain. Another shining example of sheer persistence, Macy's first four stores failed, the last one becoming bankrupt in 1855.

The irrepressible merchant was not one to accept defeat however and promptly moved to New York City to try again. His tenacity was repaid handsomely as his next business, R H Macy and Company, eventually became the largest department store in the world.

Abraham Lincoln

Perhaps one of the most inspiring stories of triumph over adversity is that of Abraham Lincoln. The sixteenth President of the United States successfully led the country through the Civil War, preserving the Union and ending slavery.

However, his path to the White House saw Lincoln overcome a succession of trials and tribulations, which included the death of his mother when he was nine; having to work as a child to help support his struggling family; several business failures; numerous election defeats; the death of his fiancé, and a nervous breakdown.

In the midst of his difficulties Lincoln was forced into bankruptcy due to the failure of his Illinois general store. His horse and saddle were seized by the sheriff, but those two assets were insufficient to cover his outstanding debt. It took Lincoln over a decade to repay the monies owed. He later admitted that debt had been his greatest life obstacle. Lincoln was a man who never accepted defeat.

In life anything is possible and sometimes it takes a dramatic turn of events to set a person upon their true path. The rich irony is that in losing some material possessions you will find a wonderful inner strength, a commodity which in itself is priceless.

11: Who Will Find Out?

Thankfully, informing people of your bankruptcy is largely something that you will not have to get involved in. From the date of the bankruptcy order you will be assigned an Official Receiver (an officer of the court appointed by the Secretary of State) who will administer the initial stages of the process.

Your Official Receiver will give notice of the bankruptcy order to various bodies including courts, bailiffs, HM Revenue and Customs, the Land Registry and any relevant professional bodies. All organisations that you have had any kind of financial relationship with will be informed and questioned, including banks and building societies, mortgage, pension and insurance companies, solicitors and landlords.

Additional enquiries will be made of any other individuals or organisations who may be able to provide details of assets or liabilities that you have, or previously had, a financial interest in. Your utility service providers may also be contacted by the Official Receiver where such accounts are provided on a credit basis.

Public Records

Your bankruptcy order will also be published in the London Gazette, which is an official publication used by organisations such as banking and credit card groups, credit reference agencies, insolvency practitioners and much of the financial industry. It will also be reported in the legal notices of a local newspaper. The purpose of this is not to 'name and shame', but merely to give any creditors not named on the bankruptcy petition the opportunity to come forward.

Details of your bankruptcy are also placed on an insolvency register maintained by the Insolvency Service and the Department for Business Enterprise and Regulatory Reform (BERR). The register contains details of current bankruptcies and those that have ended within the last three months; current individual voluntary arrangements and fast track voluntary arrangements, and current bankruptcy restriction orders and undertakings. The information held can be viewed by the public online or by visiting local Official Receivers' offices.

You are not obliged to inform your employer of your bankruptcy unless it is stipulated in your contract of employment. However, should you refuse to enter, or stop making payments under, an income payments agreement (see Chapter 27), the trustee may contact your employer to have the payments deducted from your wages directly, so in such a case your employer will find out.

12: Dealing with Creditor Harassment

When you are made bankrupt your trustee in bankruptcy takes on the responsibility to dispose of your assets and make payments to your creditors. Creditors can no longer pursue you; all claims regarding the money you owed must then be made directly to your trustee. This is to ensure that all creditors are dealt with fairly within the bankruptcy, preventing any one creditor receiving preferential treatment at the expense of the rest.

Although they should not ask you directly for payment, they may well contact you to obtain details regarding your bankruptcy and the officials who have been appointed to administer it.

Remedies for unfair creditor harassment

If you have not yet been declared bankrupt and believe you are being unfairly harassed by your creditors there are steps you can take to address the situation. Under the Administration of Justice Act 1970, harassment of people in debt by creditors or their agents is a criminal offence. Additionally, Debt Collection Guidance measures have been introduced by the Office of Fair Trading to assist consumers who are being treated unreasonably.

The guidance makes it clear that anything done by a person which is *reasonable* when trying to recover a debt is not considered to be harassment. However, creditors are warned that certain practices are considered unfair. These include: communicating in an unclear, inaccurate or misleading manner; acting with deceit; putting pressure on debtors; applying unfair charges; and acting in a threatening manner.

Taking action

If you are being subjected to any of the practices that constitute harassment, you should write to the creditor outlining your concerns about the company's behaviour. Make them aware that you are familiar with the terms of Section 40 of the Administration of Justice Act and the Office of Fair Trading Debt Collection Guidance, and request that they take steps to avoid similar occurrences in the future. Advise them how you would prefer to be contacted in future and ask that they confirm their agreement of this request.

Should your letter not have the desired effect, your next step would be to make a complaint to the trading standards department at your local council, who will investigate whether an offence has been committed and whether prosecution is appropriate. If your case of harassment involves a more serious offence, e.g. violence or blackmail, it would be pertinent to involve the police directly.

13: Sole and Joint Bank Accounts

Once declared bankrupt, your bank accounts will usually be frozen by the banks when the Official Receiver notifies them of your bankruptcy order. Effectively this means that you will not have access to them.

Any banker's cards associated with the accounts will be cancelled, along with all standing orders and direct debits. You will have to stop using any chequebooks and cards immediately and hand them over to the Official Receiver as soon as possible. Funds that are held in the accounts become an asset in the bankruptcy and are claimed by the Official Receiver. The Official Receiver may release some money to you for necessary domestic expenses. If any accounts are overdrawn, the money owed becomes a debt in the bankruptcy.

Therefore it is helpful to make preparations in advance of this action to ensure that you are not unnecessarily inconvenienced, for instance by ensuring that you have sufficient cash in hand to cover any necessary expenses. You also will need to make alternative arrangements for receiving your income and paying bills.

Some banks may allow you to keep your existing account after it has been dealt with by the Official Receiver, though they are not obliged to do so. It is unlikely that they would allow you an overdraft facility or debit card. You should make enquiries of your bank to confirm their policy.

Opening a basic bank account

An undischarged bankrupt can apply for a basic bank account. There are currently two such accounts available. The Co-operative

Bank Cashminder Account provides an Electron debit card and the Barclays Cash Card Account provides a Connect debit card. Both accounts allow you to have standing orders and offer direct debit facilities for paying regular bills.

If you intend to apply for either account you must disclose the fact that you are bankrupt. For up-to-date information on basic bank accounts you should visit the Financial Services Authority website, which is at www.moneymadeclear.fsa.gov.uk.

Dealing with joint accounts

Where you have a bank account in joint names the account will also be frozen by the bank on notification of your bankruptcy order. If there are funds available in the account, the Official Receiver will decide how much of the money to release to the joint account holder.

If the account is overdrawn, the money owed to the bank becomes a debt in the bankruptcy. In such circumstances the joint account holder will be liable to repay the total amount of money owed.

Where one party to a joint account is declared bankrupt the credit record of the other party will be affected also. Therefore, where possible, you may wish to close any joint accounts prior to the bankruptcy proceedings taking place.

Will anyone else be affected?

A bankruptcy order is listed only on your individual credit file. It will not affect the file of your partner, your children, or anyone else in your household unless you have a joint financial relationship with them.

Where a person has acted as a guarantor for a debt which is included in the bankruptcy, they will be liable for the full outstanding amount. Furthermore, your bankruptcy would affect any future applications for joint credit.

If your partner is in similar financial difficulties you are unable to make a joint petition for bankruptcy. Bankruptcy is a solution for the individual, though there is some degree of flexibility. Your partner could decide on an alternative to bankruptcy, such as an IVA, or do nothing at all if that is the best solution for them.

Create a new budget

Collecting all the details of your income and expenditure gives you the opportunity to see exactly what your financial position is on a monthly basis. Now is the ideal time to create a budget to help ensure that you can avoid similar drastic measures such as bankruptcy in the future (see Chapter 33).

By listing all of your commitments and taking them away from your total income you will have a clear picture of the amount of disposable income you have each month. Upon your discharge from bankruptcy most of your debts will be written off giving you the ideal opportunity to adopt a budget and adhere to it as closely as possible.

Of course any surplus income that you now have available will be a factor that comes under the consideration of the Official Receiver when assessing how much you can afford to contribute to the ongoing repayment of you bankruptcy debts. Where an income payments agreement (see Chapter 27) is deemed appropriate you will have to pay a percentage of any surplus income into your bankruptcy estate, usually for a period of three years.

This factor is often overlooked by people considering bankruptcy, and can provide an unwelcome sting in the tail if you have not been forewarned, so it is best to be prepared.

Part III: The Bankruptcy Process

14: The Costs

How much will it cost to make myself bankrupt?

You will be required to pay fees, currently £495. This covers:

- The court fee of £150. In certain circumstances this cost can be waived by the court, e.g. if you are on Income Support, so it is worth enquiring with the court staff whether you qualify for a reduction in the fee or are indeed exempt from the whole charge.

- £345 deposit towards the costs of administering your bankruptcy. This fee is payable in all circumstances.

- In the county court there is no fee to swear the affidavit as part of the statement of affairs. However, if your bankruptcy hearing is taking place in the High Court there is a further £7 charge. Your hearing will usually only take place at the High Court if you have resided in London for the previous six months.

If you are married and both you and your spouse are petitioning for bankruptcy, two sets of fees are payable. Fees can be paid only by cash, postal order, or by a bank, building society or solicitor's cheques. Personal cheques are not acceptable.

Getting the money together

You might find it difficult to find the money to pay the costs of the bankruptcy petition. Although saving might seem a problem, there is a solution: stop making payments to your creditors a month or two before the date you have chosen to become bankrupt.

Obviously the creditors won't be pleased and may start pressuring you to pay. However, stand firm. The sooner you have the required amount available, the sooner you can become bankrupt, at which point you will not have to deal with your creditors again.

Of course if a creditor is petitioning for your bankruptcy it is they who will pay the associated fees, it won't cost you anything.

15: Completing and Presenting Your Petition

There are two ways you can be declared bankrupt: 1. by your own petition, or 2. by the petition of one or more of your creditors.

1. Debtor's petition – making yourself bankrupt

In order to petition for your own bankruptcy you will need to complete two forms – the *petition* and *statement of affairs* – copies of which can be obtained free of charge from your local county court. The petition is form 6.27 of the Insolvency Rules 1986 and the statement of affairs is form 6.28. Another option is to download the forms and print them out to fill in, or to complete them online, by using the Insolvency Service website at www.insolvency.gov.uk. You are required to register to use the Online Form Service, and a dedicated helpline is available to assist. A feature of the Online Forms Service is that it allows the user to save and retrieve partially completed forms, as well as editing previously saved information, meaning that the daunting task of filling in all the required information can be undertaken over a number of sessions on different days.

Partially completed forms stay in the system for 90 days after the last access. The website provides information and guidance on what to include in each particular section.

Put in the work now to save pain later

Completing forms required to file for bankruptcy can be a painstaking and time consuming job. However, the time invested in completing the forms thoroughly is well worth the effort. It is your opportunity to get everything out in the open. Gathering all your bank statements, receipts, loan and credit card agreements will enable you to answer any queries fully, and in any case they will all be needed for submission to the Official Receiver following your bankruptcy order (see Chapter 17).

Submitting your forms

For online forms, you will be invited to submit them when complete. If an individual has a change of heart or circumstances, meaning they no longer wish to be made bankrupt, then no further action need be taken. The forms will remain on the system for six months, after which they will be automatically deleted if no bankruptcy order has been made.

You must either take along the completed physical forms, or printed-out copies of your online-submitted forms, when presenting your petition at court.

Once your online forms have been submitted to the Insolvency Service you cannot change any of the information online. If you notice you have made an error when completing the forms, changes must be made to the paper copies after they are printed out. When the bankruptcy order is granted you will have to inform the Official Receiver of any changes you have made.

Where you do not use the online service, you must complete your forms in capital letters using black ink. You are also required to sign and date the bottom of every page.

2. Creditor's petition – being made bankrupt by a creditor

A creditor who is owed over £750 can petition the court for your bankruptcy on the grounds that you cannot afford to pay your debts. The creditor must first serve you with a *statutory demand* for the money due. If the debt has not been paid or a settlement agreed within twenty-one days of the demand then the court will regard you as being unable to pay your debts and so will grant a bankruptcy order.

If you wish to stop the proceedings you can negotiate with the creditor in order to come to some agreement. You could also speak to an insolvency practitioner about the possibility of setting up an individual voluntary arrangement. They can then apply to have the bankruptcy proceedings set aside in the meantime whilst a meeting of creditors is called.

Of course if a creditor petitions for your bankruptcy, and it is something you want, then you do not have any court fees to pay. It is the creditor who foots the bill, which is likely to cost them around £1,500 in total. However, waiting for a creditor to instigate proceedings might not serve you well. If you have decided that bankruptcy is the right solution for you, it may be best to take the initiative and file yourself.

The court where your bankruptcy hearing will take place

It is normal practice to present your bankruptcy petition at the county court closest to where you have resided, or traded, within the last six months. If you live or trade in London your petition must be presented to the High Court. Should you live in one county but run your business in another, the bankruptcy will be dealt with where you trade.

Your local county court is listed in the phone book under 'civil courts'. In addition, Her Majesty's Courts Service website has a court finder search engine which will provide details of your local county court. This can be found at www.hmcourts-service.gov.uk. You will need to contact the court directly to discover whether it has jurisdiction to hear a bankruptcy case, and if so, to arrange a date for a hearing.

Be aware that there may be a delay of up to several weeks before your petition can be presented, depending on the volume of individual cases being heard by the court at any particular time.

If you are presenting your petition at the county court you will need to take three copies of the completed forms with you on the day of your hearing. If you are dealing with the High Court you only need to take one set.

If your bankruptcy is petitioned by one of your creditors it may be presented at the High Court in London or at a county court near where you trade or live. The fact that you are not present in England or Wales does not prevent bankruptcy proceedings being brought against you. A petition can be brought in circumstances where you are out of the country but have had residential or business connections in England or Wales within the previous three years.

Where a government department begins bankruptcy proceedings against you these may begin in the High Court in London or in one of the District Registries. However, if you have not lived or traded in the London area your case will usually be transferred to the appropriate local county court.

16: The Day of the Hearing

I encountered an unexpected delay of two weeks before the court could schedule the hearing of my own petition, due to the fact they were so busy dealing with other insolvency cases. The delay only added to my anxiety, as I was ready and willing to get the hearing over with.

When the day of the hearing finally arrived, I collected my paperwork and headed off to the county court with some degree of trepidation. I told myself that the fear of not knowing what was in store was usually far worse than the actual event, and hoped that would be true again that day.

I headed through the metal detector and was directed towards the insolvency clerk's desk. As she was already occupied, I took a seat in the waiting area and tried being calm and composed. After several minutes the person being dealt with discovered he had left his proof of Income Support at home, which he had to supply to have his £150 court fee waived.

The clerk explained that he would have to re-arrange his hearing. Unfortunately for him the next available one was not for four weeks. 'Ouch' I remember feeling. At least one way or another I was going to be dealt with that day and for that small mercy at least, I was grateful.

When my turn came, my documents were checked and thankfully all were in order. I then paid my fees in cash and swore the affidavit, which forms part of the statement of affairs, and was instructed to wait outside the courtroom until the judge was ready.

As I sat waiting, solicitors swarmed around the lobby, darting in and out of rooms. I then recognised the brother of an ex-girlfriend, who was now employed at the courts. I smiled, chatted and again tried to act like my bankruptcy hearing was an everyday occurrence, but inwardly cursed my luck at not being able to do the 'dirty deed' without being noticed!

Options open to the judge

The court judge has four different options based on the particular circumstances of your case:

- to stay the proceedings i.e. delay them, if further information is required before a bankruptcy order can be decided upon.
- to dismiss the petition, maybe because an administration order would be appropriate.
- to appoint an insolvency practitioner, if it is believed that an individual voluntary arrangement is appropriate.
- to make a bankruptcy order. In this case you will become bankrupt immediately on the making of the order.

Will you appear before the judge?

This depends on the individual judge in each court. It may be that the court clerk deals with the judge and you don't have to appear before him. Alternatively the judge may decide he or she wants to see you to ensure that you have considered all the factors involved.

In my own case I did not have to appear before the judge. The clerk advised me that the judge had already made the bankruptcy order and did not need to see me. That was a relief.

You may have an immediate telephone interview at the court

After being advised by the court clerk that I was now bankrupt I was ushered into an open-plan office where I was informed that I was required to speak to the Official Receiver's office. As I had an interest in three investment properties, the clerk was keen to ensure that my assets were brought within the Official Receiver's control as a matter of urgency.

I was handed a telephone and began answering questions on my accounts and assets. The official confirmed several of my details, being particularly concerned with how much was owed, to whom, and the details of my property portfolio. I remember getting quite frustrated as I was put on the spot regarding figures, accounts and amounts which were all detailed in the statement of affairs I had so carefully completed. However, I knew it was in my interests to co-operate fully, and did so. What seemed like 15 to 20 minutes went by until I had eventually satisfied the queries.

After I had provided as much of the information as I could, the official told me that I would have to complete a further telephone interview to investigate the circumstances behind my bankruptcy. My interview was booked for the following Monday at 11 am, and I was advised that the call would take around an hour.

I was informed that a trustee would be appointed in the interim to deal with the disposal of my assets.

With that I was free to leave the court. So, clutching my bankruptcy order in hand, I made my way to the exit and breathed a huge sigh of relief.

A major obstacle was out of the way, and I was now another bankruptcy statistic – Number 131 of 2007 in the Leeds County Court. But it mattered little. Suddenly the £66,000 worth of unsecured debt I had walked into the court with was no longer weighing heavily on my shoulders, and it felt good. I could now refer all of my creditors to the Official Receiver; my financial affairs were now completely out of my hands.

17: Official Receiver Interview

Who is the Official Receiver?

The Official Receiver is a civil servant within the Insolvency Service, and an officer of the court to which they are attached. On being notified by the court of your bankruptcy order the Official Receiver then becomes responsible for administering the initial stages of your case. Part of this involves collecting and protecting your assets and investigating the cause of your bankruptcy.

Your duties towards the Official Receiver

As a bankrupt you have a duty to comply with the Official Receiver's request to provide information about your financial affairs. This includes attending for interview as and when requested, within twenty-one days of the bankruptcy order. At this interview, you must provide documented information detailing your financial affairs. This includes: all accounting records; financial papers (e.g. bank and credit card statements, hire purchase agreements etc); your most recent set of accounts, and any other paperwork relevant to your bankruptcy. You must include a full list of assets (e.g. property, insurance policies, pensions etc), and specify the amounts of each debt and the details of which creditor they are owed to.

Although you will never be able to account for every last penny, and realistically the Official Receiver will not expect you to, it is advisable to have answers to questions about where the money has gone. Preparing well in advance could save you awkward moments later.

The process

A member of the Official Receiver's staff will contact you immediately on your becoming bankrupt if they believe that action is urgently required. If not, you will be contacted within two working days of the Official Receiver obtaining the bankruptcy order.

An interview appointment may be arranged at the Official Receiver's office. Alternatively a telephone interview may be conducted on a date agreeable to both parties. You may still opt to be interviewed in person should you prefer.

Circumstances where a telephone interview is deemed appropriate

The Official Receiver will usually offer a telephone interview where you present your own petition, have not recently traded and not previously been bankrupt.

You will then be sent a letter outlining what is expected of you. You may also be required to complete a questionnaire prior to the interview. It is in your own interests to be organised so that the process is as straightforward as possible.

Preparations prior to the interview

There are three actions to be completed by you before the interview takes place:

1. Telephone the Official Receiver immediately to confirm the interview if you have not already done so. In addition, you will also need to speak to the Official Receiver's office if:

- you require special facilities when attending the office or during the telephone interview, due to infirmity, disability or any other difficulty
- there are urgent issues that need to be sorted out
- the appointment needs to be rearranged

- you need more time to collect the paperwork or accounting records requested by the Official Receiver

2. Complete the questionnaire (if asked to do so), making a note of any points that you do not understand. The questionnaire can also be completed via the Insolvency Service website using the 'Complete your forms online' option.

3. Collect together all of the information you will need for the interview, as described earlier in this chapter.

If you are having a telephone interview, it is important that you return the completed questionnaire to the Official Receiver by the date they have requested, otherwise you may be required to attend in person.

Building rapport

Building rapport with your Official Receiver will greatly assist in making the interview as painless as possible. This begins at the first point of contact with the Official Receiver's office – which could take place immediately after your bankruptcy order is granted, as in my own case.

Once again, the more helpful and co-operative you are the smoother and speedier your bankruptcy will conclude. You will more than likely find your Official Receiver helpful and understanding. Try to relax and remember that the interview will likely be far less uncomfortable than you might fear.

It is never advisable to give into the temptation to hide anything, e.g. a debt repaid to a family member just prior to filing for bankruptcy. The Official Receiver is experienced in investigating the causes of insolvency. If it appears there have been deliberate attempts to mislead or cover up, a bankruptcy restrictions order may be imposed, extending the restrictions of bankruptcy by anything from two to fifteen years.

Interview at the Official Receiver's office

Ensure you take all the necessary documents. Your questionnaire will be checked in the private interview room, then you will be interviewed by an examiner, who is a specialist in insolvency. The examiner will question you on your assets and debts, and the facts that led to your bankruptcy.

You will be expected to explain when you applied for each specific account, what you used the funds for, and what the ongoing circumstances were around your finances for the period that your debts were built-up.

You should also hand over all of your financial records to the Official Receiver for further examination. If you have any queries you can use this opportunity to gain clarification.

An 'in person' interview can take up to three hours to complete, depending on the complexity of your circumstances.

Interview by telephone

Ensure that you have all of the relevant paperwork to hand.

The telephone interview will follow a similar format to that of the 'in person' one. The examiner will similarly want to establish the facts regarding your assets, debts and the cause of your bankruptcy, but the interview is likely to be shorter.

Will you be required to undertake a further interview?

In certain circumstances you may have to be interviewed again, particularly if the Official Receiver requires more time to complete enquiries into your affairs, or where further details regarding your assets, debts and finances are needed.

You may also be requested to undertake another interview if you cannot, or do not, provide all of the information and financial records needed by the Official Receiver.

Consequences of non-cooperation

The bankruptcy process can prove to be a complex and time-consuming journey, so anything you can do to help shorten the process has got to be worthwhile. To this end, ensuring that you co-operate fully with the Official Receiver in his administration of your assets and investigation of the cause of your bankruptcy can have the effect of reducing the time that you remain undischarged.

Moreover, if you are believed to be not co-operating fully the Official Receiver may apply to the court for your public examination. This means that you would be questioned in open court about your affairs, dealings and property, and your creditors would also have the opportunity to attend and question you.

If you have acted in a manner that may be considered worthy of a bankruptcy restriction order you could feel the temptation to try to cover it up for fear of the repercussions. However, honesty and co-operation are your key allies now. You may well be subject to some kind of sanction for a mistake you have already made, but in being open, honest and co-operative, any restriction is likely to be administered in a less damaging way.

There is also a huge amount of relief to be had in getting everything out in the open, rather than sitting on something that has the possibility of being exposed at a future date. Take your opportunity to draw a line under what has happened and move on. Dealing with the consequences immediately will allow you to enjoy your fresh start free from any lingering worries.

My own experience

I must admit I was not looking forward to my telephone interview with the Official Receiver by any stretch of the imagination. I was aware he would be assessing whether or not I had behaved recklessly and contributed to my bankruptcy, and from my own perspective I *did* feel that I was partly to blame. Throughout the previous twelve desperate months of trying to keep my head above water, I had taken on further credit to meet existing commitments. At times I had not given a clear reflection of my true financial position to my creditors, fearing that they would refuse to allow me the breathing space I needed to get on top of my situation.

Did this lack of openness mean I had acted recklessly? I was only going to find out after the Official Receiver had completed his investigations. I had already decided to continue my approach of complete honesty, even where this might result in exposing my naivety (or maybe stupidity). I had chosen this course of action and was prepared to take whatever consequences were deemed appropriate.

In the event I need not have worried. My actions weren't considered worthy of a restrictions order, and in fact I was discharged early. You may well currently be contemplating the worst-case scenario, i.e. an extension for up to fifteen years, but as my situation shows, there is probably far less to worry about than you might imagine.

Through an Internet forum I had been browsing, I was aware that many people were facing the Official Receiver interview with a fair degree of trepidation. Sometimes this fear was borne out, but more often than not those who had been through the experience had been pleasantly surprised when their worst fears were not realised.

I must confess that my own telephone interview was not as positive as some, but I took what I perceived to be the slightly condescending attitude of my interviewer on the chin. After establishing the full extent of my debt, and giving explanations how each and every one had been incurred, I was asked why I had acted so naively. I had no answer, and being made to feel like a naughty schoolboy was far from pleasant, but I figured that being chastised in this way was probably no more than I deserved. Hindsight is a wonderful thing, and at this point the folly of my actions was all too obvious to see.

As a result I allowed the examiner an easy time taking his

'power trip' for I was in no mood to take dispute with his assessment. After what seemed like an uncomfortably long period of time, but was actually only about an hour, I was advised that an insolvency practitioner would be appointed as my trustee within the week. I was left in limbo as to whether I would have to be interviewed by the Official Receiver again, being advised that it could not yet be confirmed.

With that, my 'inquisition' was over.

What happens next?

Your Official Receiver will take time to check the information you have given before compiling a report to the creditors setting out your assets and debts. The report will usually be issued within eight to twelve weeks of the bankruptcy order.

If you have significant assets, the Official Receiver is likely to seek the appointment of an insolvency practitioner to act as your trustee in bankruptcy in order to deal with the realisation and distribution of the assets. The appointment will normally be sanctioned at a meeting of creditors, or can be authorised by the Secretary of State.

When an insolvency practitioner is appointed to act as your trustee you have a duty to offer the same level of co-operation as you afford the Official Receiver in assisting with the administration of your bankruptcy estate. This includes attending for an interview as and when requested.

18: Bankruptcy Restrictions Orders

What is a bankruptcy restrictions order?

The Official Receiver has a duty to make enquiries into your bankruptcy and investigate the cause. If the enquiries indicate that you have been dishonest either before or during the bankruptcy, or that you are otherwise to blame for it, your Official Receiver can apply to the court for a *bankruptcy restrictions order* (BRO).

The court will consider the Official Receiver's report and other evidence before deciding. If it agrees, it can make an order for between two and fifteen years, during which you will continue to be subject to the restrictions of bankruptcy. Alternatively you may agree to a *bankruptcy restrictions undertaking* (BRU) which has the same effect as an order but avoids the need for court proceedings.

The restrictions

The restrictions include the following:

- If you wish to obtain credit of more than £500, you must disclose your status to the credit provider.
- Where you intend to carry on business in a different name, you must disclose to those you wish to do business with the name under which you were made bankrupt.
- You may not act as the director of a company or take part in its promotion, formation or management without first obtaining the court's permission.
- You cannot act as an insolvency practitioner, or as the receiver or manager of the property of a company on behalf of debenture holders.
- You cannot be a Member of Parliament in England or Wales.

Some restrictions are not included within insolvency law, including the inability to act as a local councillor. If you are unsure whether a BRO restricts you from being elected to or remaining in an office or position then you should contact the appointing or authorising group for guidance.

Types of behaviour considered dishonest or blameworthy

Some examples of activity that have led to the imposition of a BRO are:

- incurring debts you knew you had no chance of repaying
- giving assets away, or selling them at less than their value
- deliberately paying off certain creditors in preference to the others, e.g. friends or family
- gambling, making rash speculations, or being unreasonably extravagant
- failing to keep or produce proper records that could be used to explain any loss of money or property
- fraud, or fraudulent breach of trust
- causing the increase of debt by neglecting your business affairs
- failing to provide goods or services that have already been paid for in advance
- carrying on a business when you knew or should have been aware that you could not repay your debts

Notification of intention to apply for a BRO:

1. Within nine months of the bankruptcy order

Where the Official Receiver finalises the report to court in support of an intended application for a BRO within nine months of the bankruptcy order, they will write to inform you. This allows you twenty-one days to respond to the allegations in the report. Should you accept the Official Receiver's allegations you may offer to enter into a bankruptcy restrictions undertaking (BRU). Effectively this is exactly the same as a BRO with the exception that you do not have to attend a court hearing.

By admitting unfit conduct, the period of the BRU is likely to be shorter than a BRO. You can also put your comments to the Official Receiver which may further reduce the period.

If the Official Receiver does not receive a response to the letter within the twenty-one day period he or she will apply to the court for a BRO and write to advise you. His letter will contain a copy of the court application, the report, and supporting evidence detailing the alleged misconduct. It will also include the hearing date and the period suggested by the Official Receiver for the BRO. You must complete a form acknowledging receipt and return it to court within fourteen days.

2. After nine months of the date of the bankruptcy order

Where the Official Receiver takes longer than nine months from the date of the bankruptcy order to finalise the report, he or she will write to the court applying for a BRO and will send you a confirmatory letter at least six weeks before the court hearing date. It will include a copy of the court application, the report, and supporting evidence detailing the alleged misconduct. It will also include the hearing date and the period suggested by the Official Receiver for the BRO. Again, you must confirm receipt of the documents within fourteen days.

What happens after the BRO application has been made?

If you accept the allegations, you may enter into a BRU instead. If you wish to challenge his allegations you have a period of twenty-eight days from receiving notice to file your evidence in court. If you choose to do so, the Official Receiver may file further evidence in support of his application.

You are entitled to attend the hearing in person, take part in the proceedings, and present your own evidence regarding the case.

If you change your mind about defending the proceedings, you can still offer to enter into a BRU prior to the hearing. If you do nothing, or simply ignore the proceedings, the court will still make a BRO where it considers that the conduct reported by the Official Receiver makes this appropriate.

Length of BRO

As a general rule, if the court considers your behaviour has caused greater harm to your creditors, the BRO is likely to last longer.

Consequences for breaking the restrictions of a BRO

Failure to comply with the restrictions imposed by the court under a BRO could leave you liable to prosecution and, if found guilty, being punished with a fine or imprisonment. In addition, if you take part in the management of a company without the court's permission you will be personally responsible for any of the debts of the company that have arisen whilst you were managing it.

How long am I under threat of receiving a BRO?

Usually the Official Receiver must apply to the court for a BRO within twelve months of the bankruptcy order being made, although they can apply later with the permission of the court. In cases where the discharge from bankruptcy has been suspended, the twelve month period for making a BRO application will cease to run whilst the discharge suspension is in operation.

Where appropriate the Official Receiver may apply to the court for an interim BRO and, if granted, its restrictions will apply from the date of the interim order until the court considers the application for a BRO.

Bankruptcy annulment and a BRO

If your bankruptcy order is annulled because it should not have been made, then any BRO or BRU that is in place will automatically be annulled. All details will be removed from the public register and you will no longer be subject to any restrictions.

If the reason for the annulment of the bankruptcy order is payment of debts, or the approval of an individual voluntary arrangement or a fast-track voluntary arrangement, then the BRO or BRU will not be annulled.

19: Trustee Interview

The appointment of your 'trustee in bankruptcy'

If you have assets it is likely that the Official Receiver will seek to appoint a licensed insolvency practitioner as your trustee in bankruptcy. The trustee's main function is to realise your assets and, after paying fees and the costs involved, to distribute the remaining money to the creditors according to a strict order of priority.

A trustee will usually be appointed within four months of the order. In the meantime the Official Receiver will manage the estate. A trustee may be appointed at a later date, e.g. where assets have been acquired since the bankruptcy order, or even after the bankrupt has been discharged if there are still assets to be dealt with. You will receive notification from the Official Receiver if and when a trustee is appointed to deal with your affairs.

The Official Receiver carries the ultimate responsibility for investigating your affairs, i.e. determining whether or not you have been in some way to blame for your bankruptcy.

Seven days after my own interview with the Official Receiver, I received a letter providing details of my trustee, which informed me that from then on, any queries should directed to him.

Your legal obligations towards the trustee

Another week later, I received a letter from my trustee confirming his appointment. It set out my obligations, as defined in Sections 312 and 333 of the Insolvency Act 1986. Section 312 states the bankrupt: '... shall deliver up to the trustee possession of any

94

property, books, papers or other records of which he has possession and control and of which the trustee is required to take possession'. I was instructed to comply with this request within the following seven days.

Under Section 333 of the Act the bankrupt is also required to: '(a) give to the trustee such information as to his affairs; (b) attend on the trustee at such times; and (c) do all such things, as the trustee may for the purpose of carrying out his functions, require'. The obligations within this section apply to a bankrupt even after his discharge.

Furthermore, Section 333 also provides that if at any time after the commencement of the bankruptcy any property is acquired by the bankrupt, or there is an increase in the bankrupt's income, the bankrupt must give the trustee notice of the property or increase.

Failure to comply with any of the legal obligations set out in the above sections would render someone guilty of contempt of court and liable to be punished accordingly. I was instructed to acknowledge receipt of the letter by signing and returning an attached copy. I decided to call the trustee to confirm receipt of the letter and to make an appointment to attend their offices to undertake an interview. This was arranged for the following week. I was reminded of my duty to inform them of my present occupation and income, and of any future employment or home address changes. Subsequently, I received a letter from the trustee advising that a meeting of creditors had been arranged to agree the basis for his fee. I was not required to attend.

Functions of the trustee

The main function of the trustee is to realise and distribute the assets of the bankruptcy estate. The trustee has a duty to the creditors to dispose of the assets for the best possible price, enabling the creditors to receive as large a share of the assets as possible after the fees, costs and expenses of the bankruptcy have been paid.

The trustee can apply to the court for an order restoring property which a bankrupt has disposed of in a way that is unfair to their creditors, e.g. if before the bankruptcy order, a property has been transferred to a relative for less than its full value.

The trustee can claim property obtained by a bankrupt during the bankruptcy, and can arrange an income payments agreement or order which would require the bankrupt to pay some surplus income for a period of up to three years (see Chapter 27).

Powers of the trustee

A creditors committee can be appointed at a meeting of creditors. It consists of three to five elected creditors and its purpose is to protect and promote all creditors' interests. The trustee must write a report for the committee at least once every six months, and keep financial records for the bankruptcy which are open to inspection by the committee.

The trustee has certain powers which can be used only with permission of the court, or creditor's committee where appointed:

- to carry on the business of the bankrupt so far as may be necessary for the benefit of the creditors
- to bring or defend legal actions relating to the property of the bankrupt
- to come to a compromise with creditors of the bankrupt about their debts
- to sell the property of the bankrupt for a sum of money payable in the future
- to mortgage the property of the bankrupt to raise money to pay the bankrupt's debts

Additionally the trustee has powers that need no permission:

- to sell the property of the bankrupt, providing it is not for a sum of money payable in the future
- to act and to sign documents in the name and on behalf of the bankrupt

- to employ an agent
- to do everything necessary to wind up the bankrupt's affairs

My own trustee interview

Although I resided in Leeds at the time of my bankruptcy the insolvency practitioner that was appointed as trustee was based in York. Therefore I had to make my way to York to attend my interview. I was feeling slightly more at ease than I did prior to my Official Receiver interview, assuring myself it would not be as difficult. Nevertheless, I was eager to get this next major hurdle out of the way.

As it turned out there was nothing to be unduly worried about. The person who was dealing with my case on behalf of the trustee merely took me through the process of detailing all of my income, assets, debts and creditors. I found this more than a little frustrating as I had first supplied all this information in my statement of affairs, confirmed it during my telephone conversation with the Official Receiver's office after my court hearing, and had been required to go through it yet again during my actual telephone interview with the Official Receiver.

However, I again stuck to my approach of 'full co-operation' knowing that another significant part of my bankruptcy experience was soon to be over. I was advised that as I had equity available in my investment properties the trustee was under an obligation to realise this. The properties, which I co-owned with a joint investor, were to be independently valued so that the amount of equity that made up my interest in the properties could be determined.

The trustee would then look to realise the equity by selling them to the joint investor, if a suitable price could be agreed, or by applying to the court for an order for the sale of the properties. I was advised that I would be kept updated with the progress, and left the trustee's office having again given my complete co-operation.

It was some three months later before I heard from the trustee's office again. A letter arrived informing me of the details of the valuations and how much my interest in the properties amounted to. The trustee enquired whether I wanted, or was in a position, to make an offer to purchase the interest in the properties.

I broke into a wry smile, amused at the irony of asking a bankrupt if he had a significant sum of money available to invest in properties! I replied that I would not be in a position to make such an offer.

The trustee then began negotiations with the joint investor regarding the purchase of my beneficial interests. If no agreement could be reached the trustee intended to seek a court order for possession and sale of the properties. In the event a compromise was reached that was agreeable to both parties.

Part IV: While You Are Undischarged

20: Duties and Restrictions

The duties of a bankrupt

After you have become subject to a bankruptcy order there are certain duties that you must comply with:

You must cease using any bank, building society, credit card or similar accounts immediately, and cannot make any payments directly to your creditors in respect of any of the debts included in the bankruptcy (subject to certain exceptions. See Chapter 22).

Whilst subject to the bankruptcy order you are legally bound to inform your trustee about any assets and increases in income that you acquire during your bankruptcy, e.g. any lump sum payments received such as redundancy or an inheritance received from a will.

You may also be required to attend court to explain the circumstances that caused your bankruptcy. Failure to comply with such a request could lead to arrest.

The restrictions placed on a bankrupt

An undischarged bankrupt cannot engage in certain activities. You commit a criminal offence if you take part in any of the following:

• Obtaining credit of £500 or more either alone or jointly with any other person without disclosing your bankruptcy. This provision includes getting credit by words or actions intended to obtain credit, even though you have not made a specific credit agreement, e.g. ordering goods and then refusing to pay for them

• Carrying on a business, either directly or indirectly, in a name different from that in which you were made bankrupt, without telling all of those who you do business with the name in which you were made bankrupt

- Being directly or indirectly concerned in promoting, forming or managing a limited company, or acting as a company director, without the court's permission. This applies whether you are formally appointed director or not

Other restrictions not covered by insolvency law include the inability to hold certain public offices, as well as holding office as trustee of a charity or a pension fund (see Chapter 26). If you are unsure of whether or not your own circumstances may cause a breach of the bankruptcy restrictions you should call the Insolvency Service Enquiry Line for further guidance on 0845 602 9848.

Restrictions regarding new accounts

You may open a new bank or building society account after the bankruptcy order, but you must inform them that you are bankrupt and they may impose conditions and limitations. You must not obtain overdraft facilities without disclosing your bankruptcy and should not write any cheques that are likely to be dishonoured.

As you are going about the business of repairing your credit report and financial standing it is in your interests to use all facilities responsibly and within the agreements laid out. Financial institutions will pay close attention to how you have managed your accounts since bankruptcy when assessing future requests for banking facilities or borrowing.

You are required to inform your trustee about any money that you have in your account which is more than you need for your reasonable living expenses. The trustee has the ability to claim any surplus amounts to pay your creditors.

How long will the restrictions last?

You will be freed from the restrictions upon your discharge from bankruptcy. You also automatically become free from the restrictions of bankruptcy in circumstances where the court annuls (cancels) the bankruptcy order (see Chapter 21).

However, if you have not complied with your duties as a bankrupt your trustee can apply to the court for your discharge to be postponed. Should the court agree, your bankruptcy will only end when the suspension has been lifted and the remaining time on your bankruptcy period has expired.

21: Annulment and the Fast Track Voluntary Arrangement

Annulment

Annulment of bankruptcy is a procedure by which a court cancels the bankruptcy order. You can apply to the court for an *order of annulment* at any time where:

• the bankruptcy order should not have been made, e.g. because the proper steps were not taken.

• all of your bankruptcy debts and the fees and expenses of the bankruptcy proceedings have either been paid in full or secured (guaranteed) to the court.

• you have agreed an IVA with your creditors to repay all or part of your debts.

Effects

An annulment means that, in law, the bankruptcy order was never made. You revert to your pre-bankruptcy status. Any disposals of your property by the trustee in bankruptcy will remain valid and will not be reversed. Any assets remaining will be returned to you and you will be liable for any of your debts that have not been paid in the bankruptcy.

Co-operating with the Official Receiver

Even if you have applied for annulment you should still attend your Official Receiver interview and provide any information you are asked for. The court might not annul the bankruptcy order until the Official Receiver confirms that you have done so.

Stopping the bankruptcy being advertised

The Official Receiver must advertise a bankruptcy in the London Gazette along with another newspaper, and these actions can only be prevented by a court order. Therefore, if you are applying for an annulment you may be able to apply to the court for a 'stay of advertisement', but you must act immediately. You should telephone the court and inform them that you wish to apply for a stay of advertisement of the bankruptcy order. You should also advise the Official Receiver that you are making the application.

Fast Track Voluntary Arrangement

If you have been made bankrupt by one of your creditors but believe that you can provide a significantly better return to your creditors than they will otherwise receive through your bankruptcy, then by entering into a Fast Track Voluntary Arrangement (FTVA) you can get your bankruptcy annulled.

An FTVA is a binding agreement made between you and your creditors to pay all or part of the money you owe. It can only be entered into after you have been made bankrupt. In order to enter into an FTVA you must secure the co-operation of your Official Receiver, who will act as your nominee. Their role is to help you prepare your proposal to put to your creditors.

For the FTV to be accepted, 75 percent of the creditors who vote must agree to the proposal. It is then legally binding, and no creditor can take legal action regarding the debt providing you keep to the agreement. As nominee, your Official Receiver will then supervise the arrangement, making payments to your creditors in accordance with your proposals.

Costs

The Official Receiver's fee for acting as nominee is £310. Additionally, for carrying out the ongoing role of supervisor of the

FTVA, the Official Receiver will charge fifteen percent of monies from any assets you own or any money collected from you. You will also be required to pay a £10 registration fee for your FTVA to be recorded on the public register of individual voluntary arrangements.

Duration

There is no fixed time period for an FTVA. The length of time it lasts will be outlined in your proposal. You may offer to make regular payments from your income for a specified number of years. For your Official Receiver to agree to act as nominee you must be able to offer a return to your creditors that is significantly better than they would obtain through your bankruptcy. Thus the agreement may well extend beyond the three-year period of an IPA, for instance (see Chapter 27).

Effects of the FTVA on your bankruptcy

Once the FTVA has been agreed your Official Receiver will apply to have your bankruptcy order annulled, i.e. voided, as if it had never existed. This usually occurs around five to seven weeks after the FTVA has begun. You will then no longer be subject to the restrictions of the bankruptcy order. If any assets have not been included in your FTVA for distribution to your creditors, e.g. your home, they will then be returned to you.

Failure to comply with the FTVA

Should you fail to keep up the agreed payments or deliver up any assets included in the proposal then the FTVA will fail. Where you have deliberately not complied with the terms of the agreement the Official Receiver will make you bankrupt again. If the failure is caused by circumstances beyond your control, e.g. redundancy, the Official Receiver will take no further action against you. However, your creditors can take action against you to recover the monies you owe, which may include petitioning for your bankruptcy.

Amendment of public records

• Individual Insolvency Register – when a bankruptcy order is annulled the record of the order will be removed from the register immediately.

• HM Land Registry – you can ask the court to include in an order of annulment the fact that any registration of the bankruptcy petition or order at the Land Charges Department should be cancelled. You should then contact the Land Charges Department to ask for cancellation. Restriction notices may also have been registered against the title to the property. You can apply in writing to the Land Registry office that serves your area to have these entries removed.

• Credit reference agencies – it is your responsibility to have details of the bankruptcy order removed from your credit file.

• Notifications – if the Official Receiver has informed anyone about the bankruptcy order, he or she will also notify them of an annulment.

22: Deciding which Bills to Pay

On being declared bankrupt you have a general duty not to make any payments directly to your creditors (see Chapter 12).

However, there are certain types of debt which are not included within bankruptcy proceedings, and therefore must continue to be paid:

- **Secured debt**

Where a debt remains secured on the asset in question, e.g. a property, it is still enforceable. Secured creditors should continue to be paid in accordance with the terms of your agreement with them. If you fail to keep up your mortgage repayments and fall into arrears the lender may repossess your home.

- **Non-provable debt**

Certain types of debt are referred to as *non-provable*, meaning that they are not written off by bankruptcy proceedings. Therefore you will remain liable for such debts regardless of your bankruptcy.

Examples of non-provable debts include court fines, matrimonial settlements, maintenance orders and CSA payments. Debts that have arisen from fraudulent conduct are also excluded from your bankruptcy. You will only be released from a liability to pay damages to a person for personal injury if the court thinks fit.

- **Overpayment of benefits and tax credits**

The benefit provider can recover overpayments from any further benefits you receive until you are discharged, at which point you will be released from such debts.

- **Student loans**

Since 1 September 2004, all outstanding student loans are excluded from bankruptcy and must be paid as per the terms of the agreement. Where you are currently having payments taken directly from your salary these will continue until the loan is repaid. If you fall below the income threshold, no payments will be made until your salary reaches the level where repayments automatically begin. Interest will continue to accrue in the meantime.

If you were made bankrupt prior to 1 September 2004, you should seek clarification from your Official Receiver, as you may still be liable for the repayment of your loan.

- **Rent and rent arrears**

You must continue to pay any continuing commitments such as your rent. Any rent arrears outstanding at the time of the petition must be included in the bankruptcy. After you have been declared bankrupt, you cannot pay your rent arrears in order to safeguard your house without getting the express permission of your Official Receiver. It is for your Official Receiver to decide whether or not you can afford to pay any money from your income towards any of your debts (including rent arrears).

Your arrears may put you in breach of contract with your landlord who can seek to evict you. This action is less likely if you are a housing association tenant but it still remains a possibility. If the housing association does apply to the county court for an order to evict it then becomes a matter for the court to decide.

- **Utility bills**

Companies who supply the gas, electricity, water and telephone services to your home cannot demand payment of any bills in your name which are unpaid at the date of the bankruptcy order. However, they may require you to pay a deposit for further supplies, and have the accounts transferred into the name of your spouse or partner.

If you are unsure about whether or not you should continue to repay any debt you should seek clarification from your Official Receiver before proceeding.

23: The Effect on Your Assets

From the date of the bankruptcy order, the Official Receiver takes responsibility for protecting your assets. Usually the Official Receiver will arrange for an insolvency practitioner to be appointed as your trustee in bankruptcy. The trustee will then deal with realising any assets of value, using the proceeds to first recover the costs of the bankruptcy proceedings, and then to distribute any remaining funds between your creditors.

Ultimately the trustee will decide which assets you can and cannot keep, though it is very unlikely that you will be able to keep anything of significant value. It is your duty to provide the trustee with details of all of your assets. Where an 'essential' item's worth isn't greater than the cost of a reasonable replacement, eg a car, then it will not be included in the bankruptcy.

1. Exempt Assets that May be Kept

Exempt property does not form part of the bankruptcy estate and is therefore not automatically available to the trustee to realise on behalf of the creditors. Two main categories of property are defined as exempt in Section 283(2) of the Insolvency Act 1986:

a) Household items – clothing, bedding, furniture, household equipment and provisions necessary to satisfy the basic domestic needs of the bankrupt and his or her family. Household items will rarely be claimed and sold by the trustee as they generally have little second hand value. Where the trustee is aware that the bankrupt's home contains items of a high resale value such as antiques, these will be claimed for the estate.

Technically items in the home such as computer equipment, stereos, televisions etc are not exempt assets as they are not necessary to satisfy basic domestic needs, although they may be exempt if they are required for the business or employment needs of the bankrupt. However, such items will usually have little second hand value and will rarely be claimed for the estate.

b) Employment / business items – includes tools, books, vehicles and other equipment necessary for the personal use of the bankrupt to continue his or her employment, business or vocation. Any such item must be necessary for the bankrupt's personal use for it to be considered as exempt. The item does not have to be for the exclusive use of the bankrupt, but where it is for use by a spouse or employees and not by the bankrupt it will not be treated as exempt. Each case is considered on its own merits.

Motor vehicles may be exempted if they are necessary for the personal use of the bankrupt in his or her business, employment or vocation or where they are necessary to meet the basic domestic needs of the bankrupt and his or her family (see Chapter 25).

In addition, several other types of assets may be exempted:

• **Pensions** – you should inform your trustee about all your pension arrangements. Pension schemes that have been approved by HM Revenue and Customs cannot usually be claimed as an asset in your bankruptcy. Other kinds of pensions can also be excluded (see Chapter 28). If you are unsure about a particular pension scheme you should seek further guidance from the Insolvency Service or your trustee.

• **Student loan funds** – Where you are in possession of funds from a student loan, and the balance of the loan remains payable, the loan funds will not be included within the bankruptcy.

- **Bankrupt's right to claim property as exempt** – As a bankrupt you have the right to claim that an item is necessary for your family's basic domestic needs, or to carry out your employment. It is for the bankrupt to prove that the item being claimed is necessary and therefore should be treated as exempt.

2. Assets You May Lose

There are certain assets the trustee has authority to dispose of without your consent, including any items which are not considered to be exempt. The following list is not exhaustive but will provide some idea of the assets that may be realised by the trustee to pay your creditors:

- **Beneficial interest in your home** – if you own your home the beneficial interest in it will form part of your bankruptcy estate, even where it is jointly owned. It may be that the home has to be sold to go towards paying your debts. Your partner, a relative or friend may be able to buy your interest in the home from the trustee (see Chapter 24).

- **Credit balances, savings and investments** - credit balances in bank or building society accounts become assets in the bankruptcy, as do investments held in shares, bonds, endowments and savings policies.

- **Exempt property of excess value** – The trustee has a right to claim exempt property if he or she is of the opinion that it could be sold, replaced by one of lower cost and produce a surplus for the estate.

- **Surplus income** - where you have a surplus income after essential expenditure, your trustee may apply to the court for an income payments order, requiring you to make contributions towards the bankruptcy debts from your income. Such an order will not be made by the court if it would leave you without enough income to meet the reasonable domestic needs of you and your family. Payments under such an order continue for a maximum of three years from the date the order is made and can continue after you have been discharged from bankruptcy. If you receive payments from a pension before your discharge from bankruptcy, they can be included in any calculation for an income payments agreement (see Chapter 27). This applies whether your pension is exempted from the bankruptcy or not (Chapter 28).

- **Business assets not exempted** – a bankrupt cannot claim stock or business premises as exempt property under any circumstances. Such assets will be part of the bankruptcy estate and realised by the trustee.

- **Life assurance policy** – generally any interest you have in a life assurance policy will be claimed as an asset in the bankruptcy. Your trustee may be entitled to sell or surrender the policy in order to collect any proceeds on behalf of your creditors. If the policy is held in joint names the other party should contact the trustee to agree a way forward regarding how their interest in the policy will be dealt with. It may be possible for your interest to be transferred for an amount equal to the current value of it. If the life assurance policy has been legally charged to any creditor, e.g. an endowment policy used as security for the mortgage on your home, the rights of the secured creditor will not be affected by the making of the bankruptcy order. However, any remaining value in the policy may be claimed by the trustee.

- **Assets disposed of** - if the trustee believes you have disposed of any asset in a way which was unfair to your creditors, e.g. transferring property to a friend for an amount less than it is worth, he or she can apply to the court for an order reclaiming the asset.

- **Newly acquired assets** - you are under a duty to advise your trustee of any asset that you acquire during the term of your bankruptcy, e.g. lottery wins or an inheritance received via a will. He may then realise it for the benefit of your creditors. Any other monies received after the date of bankruptcy but before the date of your discharge may also be claimed at the discretion of the trustee.

- **Ongoing / pending court claims** - where you have an ongoing claim against another person through court proceedings, or where you think you may have a claim (a right of action) against another person, the claim may become an asset in your bankruptcy.

24: Saving Your Home

If you own your home, your interest in it will form part of your bankruptcy estate which will be dealt with by your trustee, whether it is freehold or leasehold, solely or jointly owned, mortgaged or otherwise. Your home may have to be sold to go towards the payment of your debts.

Your mortgage lender will be informed of the trustee's interest in the property, and therefore of your bankruptcy. This will occur whether your mortgage is in arrears or not.

If your home is mortgaged and you fall behind with payments, then your lender may seek repossession. It is advisable to keep your mortgage lender informed about your bankruptcy so that all possible options can be considered at the earliest opportunity.

Delaying the sale of your home

The property will be sold by the trustee where it is the only way that money can be released to your creditors. If you have a spouse or children living with you, it may be possible for the sale to be put off until after the end of the first year of bankruptcy.

This extra time will enable alternative housing arrangements to be made. If the trustee still retains an interest in the property after this period the court will only prevent an order for sale in exceptional circumstances, or where your interest in the property is worth less than £1,000.

Preventing the sale of your home

Another interested party may be able to buy the interest in your home from the trustee, and in doing so would prevent a sale of the property by the trustee at a future date. This can occur even where the interest is very small, worth nothing, or you owe more on the property than it is currently worth. The other interested party should take legal advice about the property as soon as possible if such a situation applies.

The beneficial interest

Your beneficial interest in the property is the amount you will usually receive from the sale proceeds. It is separate from the legal title to the property, which is held by the owner. If you are the sole owner of the home the beneficial interest is the whole value of the property. Where the property is jointly owned the beneficial interest is usually an equal share of the value.

Any amounts owed on mortgages or other loans secured on the home are repaid first from the sale proceeds. The beneficial interest is calculated after deducting such amounts.

Your beneficial interest in the property transfers to the Official Receiver on the date of your bankruptcy order. Where an insolvency practitioner is subsequently appointed as your trustee the beneficial interest is then automatically transferred to him or her.

If you are the sole owner of the property the legal title will also be transferred. Where the property is jointly owned the legal title remains with you and the co-owner, however, the trustee in bankruptcy is still free to take action in relation to the property, e.g. applying for an order for possession or sale.

The trustee in bankruptcy can consider selling the beneficial interest to a partner, a relative or a friend, which may allow you to remain in the property.

Solely owned properties and the bankruptcy restriction notice

Where a property is solely owned by a bankrupt, a bankruptcy restriction notice will be entered against the property at the Land Registry. The restriction is automatically placed when the bankruptcy order is made, recording that the bankrupt is no longer the legal owner of the property and is not able to enter into any dealings in connection with it.

The restriction will only be removed once the trustee has been paid his legal and beneficial interest in the property. If the interest in the property gets returned to you, the trustee will inform the Chief Land Registrar that the property is now yours again.

Jointly owned properties and the Form J restriction

Where a property is jointly owned by a bankrupt, the trustee will apply for a Form J restriction to be entered at the Land Registry. This records the trustee's beneficial interest in the property. It requires the Land Registry to notify the trustee of any dealings in relation to the property. The restriction differs from a *charge*, which relates to a claim for a specific amount of money.

With a jointly owned property a bankrupt's legal interest does not transfer to the trustee. Therefore the bankrupt and co-owner can still sell the property, although the trustee must be paid the value of the beneficial interest from the sale proceeds.

A Form J restriction is only removed once the trustee has been paid his beneficial interest in the property. If the property is sold the trustee will make a claim against the property.

Valuation of the trustee's claim

Where a Form J restriction has been registered, the value of the trustee's claim is simply the value of the trustee's beneficial interest in the property. Therefore this value is subject to change, depending on the value of the property and any amounts owed on mortgages and other charges secured on the home.

The trustee may be able to claim the full amount of the beneficial interest even if the value of it is more than the costs, fees and debts owed in the bankruptcy. This is due to the fact that creditors are entitled to interest when there are enough assets in the bankruptcy.

Where the value of the beneficial interest is less than the costs, fees and debts owed, the trustee need only be paid the value of the beneficial interest to release the Form J restriction.

Purchasing the beneficial interest in a jointly owned property

Where your trustee in bankruptcy is the Official Receiver, any interested party may be able to purchase the beneficial interest by taking part in a property conveyancing scheme run by the Insolvency Service and a firm of solicitors. The scheme allows the beneficial interest to be transferred back to you, or the beneficial interest and legal title can be transferred to the other party.

There are fees to pay (currently £211) to cover the Official Receiver's costs. In addition the cost of an individual valuation will have to be paid, along with the agreed purchase price for the beneficial interest based on the valuation. If the home is now worth less than the amount owed on it, the price of the beneficial interest will be set at £1. If you wish to take part in the scheme you should contact your Official Receiver for further details.

If your trustee is an insolvency practitioner the other interested party should contact them for information about purchasing the beneficial interest.

Purchasing the beneficial interest in a solely owned property

Your trustee can transfer both the beneficial interest and legal title to you (usually after your discharge from bankruptcy) or to your partner, relative or friend, but the transaction is more complicated where the property is solely owned. There is no fixed-price property conveyancing scheme but similar costs will have to be paid. You should contact your trustee for further details.

What happens if the beneficial interest in not purchased?

If no-one buys the beneficial interest it will remain with your trustee in bankruptcy for a set period of time – it does not return to you upon discharge.

The value of the beneficial interest may increase over time if the market value of your home increases, and any such increase will go to your trustee to pay your debts, even if the home is sold some time after you have been discharged. You and your family will be required to move out of the home if it has to be sold.

If the trustee is initially unable to sell your home he or she may obtain a charging order on your interest in it, but only if that interest is worth more than £1,000. Where a charging order is obtained, your interest in the property will be returned to you, but the legal charge over the interest will remain. The amount covered by the legal charge will be the total value of your interest in the property. This sum must be paid from your share of the proceeds when you sell the property.

Will you have the beneficial interest returned to you?

In most cases, where the trustee is aware of your interest in the property and the interest has not been sold by the third anniversary of your bankruptcy, it will no longer be part of your bankruptcy estate and will be returned to you.

The exceptions to this are: where your trustee has applied for an order for the sale; your trustee has applied for an order for possession; your trustee has applied for an order imposing a charge on the house; or where you and the trustee agree that you will incur a specified liability in respect of the beneficial interest.

If the trustee has not previously been made aware of your interest in a property, he or she has a three-year period in which to deal with it, starting from the date the interest is notified.

Will you have to sell your endowment policy?

This depends on whether the endowment policy has been assigned to a bank or building society as security for a mortgage. Where it is so assigned it will not be possible for the trustee in bankruptcy to sell it, as the rights to the proceeds of the policy no longer belong to you.

The downside of this is that the level of outstanding mortgage owed will reduce in line with the value of the endowment, and so there will be an increase in the value of the equity available in the property.

If the endowment policy is not assigned to a lender the trustee will be able to enforce the sale of the policy in order to release the funds to pay your creditors. Whether or not this action is taken is at the sole discretion of the trustee.

If you require advice regarding housing problems you should contact Shelter, the housing advice charity (see Chapter 8).

Property rental and bankruptcy

It is likely that your Official Receiver or trustee will inform your landlord of your bankruptcy. Whether this will affect your tenancy depends on the terms of your tenancy agreement. If you are unsure what the position is, you should seek legal advice. If you would like to try to prevent your landlord finding out, it is advisable for you to contact your Official Receiver or trustee to try and agree a way forward.

Your trustee in bankruptcy will want to confirm the amount of your rent payment by obtaining details from your landlord. However, it may be that the trustee will accept other proof of the amount you are paying, e.g. a bank statement.

It is not your trustee's intention to make matters difficult for you, and so if you are genuinely concerned that your bankruptcy may result in the termination of your tenancy, take the bull by the horns and speak to your trustee.

However, if you have rent arrears, the debt will be included in the bankruptcy. As such your landlord becomes a creditor and will automatically be informed about the bankruptcy order. If you wish to remain in the property, you will have to come to an agreement with your landlord regarding the arrears. Whether or not the Official Receiver will allow you to pay any arrears is another matter.

Future property rental

If you apply to rent property via a letting agent they may perform a credit check and you could be declined because of your bankruptcy. Many private landlords do not check credit so you should still be able to enter into a tenancy agreement using a private landlord.

25: Keeping Your Motor Vehicle

After making the decision to file for bankruptcy one of the first questions usually asked is: 'will I lose my car?' The answer depends on whether you can prove that the vehicle is necessary for your *employment, business or vocation* or for satisfying the basic domestic needs of you and your family.

Employment, business or vocation

In deciding whether or not the bankrupt's vehicle is necessary for the individual's personal use in the course of his employment, business or vocation the Official Receiver will take account of the following significant factors:

- Is the vehicle used by the bankrupt in his employment, business or vocation?
- Can the bankrupt reasonably travel to and from his place of employment without the vehicle?
- Would the bankrupt's prospects of obtaining employment diminish without use of the vehicle, even though the bankrupt may not specifically be in employment at the date of the bankruptcy order? In such cases, the Official Receiver must consider whether there is a reasonable prospect of the bankrupt obtaining work.
- A self-employed bankrupt who is unemployed at the date of the bankruptcy order may be able to retain a vehicle as an exempt asset if the individual can satisfy the Official Receiver that there is a reasonable prospect of them obtaining work.
- Would the bankrupt's prospect of obtaining work diminish even if the vehicle requires repair, as it will then be used to travel to work or to seek employment once repaired?

The definition 'employment, business or vocation' has been widened to include informal full-time carers of a disabled friend or relative who would use the vehicle in connection with that role.

If the bankrupt is unable to convince the Official Receiver that the vehicle is necessary for his employment, business or vocation, it may be treated as part of the estate and dealt with accordingly.

Domestic needs

The Official Receiver may treat the motor vehicle as exempt where the bankrupt can show that it is necessary for domestic use (e.g. for taking children to and from school), or where the bankrupt suffers from a disability which makes the vehicle necessary.

Such cases are required to be treated sympathetically. However, it is for the bankrupt to convince the Official Receiver that the motor vehicle is necessary; that no practical alternative exists; that it meets a genuine need and is not simply a matter of convenience.

A bankrupt living in an urban area with reasonable transport links is unlikely (other than as a result of disability) to be in a position to claim that a motor vehicle is necessary to meet domestic need. The individual will have to demonstrate that there is no public transport alternative or that the distance to travel would make walking (or cycling) an impractical alternative. It is not sufficient for a bankrupt who lives in a rural area to claim a motor vehicle simply by virtue of distance from a school, for instance.

Where a bankrupt's disability would prevent them seeking employment, the Official Receiver needs to be satisfied that the vehicle allows the bankrupt a degree of independent living which would be impossible without keeping the vehicle, and/or that there is no practical alternative to allow the bankrupt to undertake routine medical appointments or care associated with his disability.

In reality, the question of whether or not a vehicle is exempt property can be a difficult one. The Official Receiver will use their discretion in considering each case according to its merits within the guidelines issued to him.

Exempt but of 'excess value'

Where a vehicle is exempted, the Official Receiver may claim it for the estate if they consider that the realisable value of the vehicle exceeds the cost of a more economic replacement, i.e. the car is an expensive model. Steps to claim an exempt vehicle will be taken where the potential net realisation to the estate is at least £500 after taking into account costs of sale and of a replacement vehicle.

However, the nature of the bankrupt's business is an important consideration for the Official Receiver. Where the bankrupt can show the need to retain a high value vehicle which is integral to the business, e.g. as a chauffeur, then exemption for the vehicle might be obtained.

Valuing and replacing an 'excess value' vehicle

To obtain an accurate valuation of the vehicle in question the Official Receiver can rely on 'Parker's Guide'. This is an independent vehicle valuing service used by motor traders and the insurance industry. It can be accessed at www.parkers.co.uk.

Under Section 308 of the Insolvency Act 1986 a guideline maximum figure of £2000 was introduced when deciding on an allowance for a replacement vehicle. Although this limit remains today, it can be exceeded in circumstances where there are strong arguments for doing so.

Outstanding finance

Where a vehicle is subject to a financial agreement, the Official Receiver will contact the hiring owner. Once the value of any equity is known, a decision will then be made as to whether there would be a benefit to the estate in realising the vehicle.

If there is deemed to be no benefit in realising the vehicle the issue is then whether the finance company are still prepared to deal with the bankrupt. Most hire purchase companies would rather receive a monthly payment for the duration of the agreement. This is preferable to them than taking the car back, selling it at a loss, and then claiming in the bankruptcy only to receive nothing.

Disposal

Where a vehicle is not exempt but the bankrupt has expressed a wish to keep it, it is a general policy that the Official Receiver will attempt to reach agreement with the bankrupt for the sale of the vehicle to him.

26: Present and Future Employment

1. Employed (Will my employer find out?)

Official Advertisement

You are not obliged to inform your employer about your bankruptcy unless it is stipulated in your contract of employment. However, as your bankruptcy is advertised in the London Gazette and a local newspaper it is possible your employer may find out.

'nil tax code'

If you pay tax under the PAYE system HM Revenue and Customs will usually apply a 'nil tax' code to you for the rest of the tax year in which you were declared bankrupt. The effect of this is to instruct the individual's employer not to take any more income tax from their wages for the rest of the tax year.

HMRC applies nil tax codes for various reasons, including overpayment of taxes in previous years or in other employment, and as such the new code will not show the employer that the individual is bankrupt. However, should you fail to make payments required under an income payments order (see Chapter 27), the trustee may contact your employer to have the amount deducted from your wages directly and this will, of course, inform him of your status.

Implications for your current employment

If you are a member of a professional body, your bankruptcy may result in the loss of your membership, which could mean you are unable to continue in your current role. In some other professions, dismissal will be at the discretion of your employer. You should check the terms of your contract of employment or consult your Human Resources department or union for further clarification.

Your bankruptcy order may also affect any registration, licence or permission you hold in connection with your work. Where you are unsure, you should contact the person who issued the registration or authority to establish if it will remain in force or will be cancelled or withdrawn.

My own experience of informing my employer

In deciding to opt for bankruptcy I had fully prepared myself for the fact that I would lose my job. I had been working as a clerical officer for the Royal Bank of Scotland and, under the terms of my employment contract, bankruptcy was considered gross misconduct.

It was Christmas 2006, a week after I had made the decision to become bankrupt. On the evening of Boxing Day I wrote my resignation, to be handed in first thing the next morning.

I arrived at work one hour early hoping to find the manager on his own. To my relief he was. I explained my situation and told him I was fully aware of the consequences. To my surprise the manager advised me that he would explore the possibility of saving my job.

However, I had already made peace with the fact that I would be leaving, and I wanted to go on my own terms rather than cling to some hope that might turn out to be false. The manager accepted my decision, and considerately arranged for me to have my four weeks' notice period paid in full.

Employment restrictions

The Enterprise Act 2002 introduced bankruptcy restrictions orders, and in doing so changed the effect of bankruptcy on certain types of employment. As a result some restrictions now apply to undischarged bankrupts whilst others only apply to individuals against whom a bankruptcy restriction order (BRO) is in place.

Some of the main employment restrictions imposed by bankruptcy are covered here. This list is by no means definitive and should be used for guidance only. Where you are unsure of how bankruptcy will affect you personally you should always seek clarification from the relevant advisory body.

- Insolvency practitioner – a bankrupt may not act as an insolvency practitioner before being discharged from bankruptcy or whilst there is a BRO in force.

- House of Commons / House of Lords – an individual subject to a BRO is disqualified from sitting or voting in the House of Lords; being elected to, sitting or voting in the House of Commons, or sitting or voting in a committee in either House, for the duration of the BRO.

- Solicitors – Under Section 15 of the Solicitors Act 1974 any current practising certificate held by a solicitor is immediately suspended on the making of a bankruptcy order. However, The Law Society may lift the suspension. No such restriction is placed on a practising barrister although the Bar Council should be informed.

- Trustee of a charity – an individual subject to a BRO is disqualified from acting as the trustee of a charity.

- Estate agents – both an undischarged bankrupt and an individual subject to a BRO are disqualified from engaging in estate agency work of any sort otherwise than as an employee of another person.

- School governors – an individual subject to a BRO will be disqualified from holding office, or continuing to hold office, as a school governor.

- Local government councillor – an undischarged bankrupt is disqualified from holding office in local government if there is a BRO in force against him.

- Pensions – an undischarged bankrupt, or a discharged bankrupt subject to a BRO, is disqualified from being a trustee of any trust scheme, unless the disqualification is waived by the Occupational Pensions Regulatory Authority.

- The armed forces – under the rules for enlistment in the Army, Navy and RAF, a bankrupt is not permitted to enlist while they remain undischarged from bankruptcy.

- Fit and proper person – Various regulations, bye-laws and private club rules refer to the individual being a 'fit and proper person', e.g. when applying to the local police for a taxi licence. It may be that an individual subject to a BRO is not considered a 'fit and proper person' within the terms of the definition for certain occupations or membership.

Getting employment whilst undischarged

Whilst bankrupt, you are under a duty to tell your trustee about any increases in income you obtain during your bankruptcy. You must also inform your trustee of any property which becomes yours during the bankruptcy, e.g. redundancy payments.

If you begin employment whilst undischarged the trustee will want to assess the possibility of an income payments agreement, which can only be put in place before you are discharged, and can run for a period of three years. It is important that you continue to co-operate fully by providing any relevant information.

When NOT to be open about your bankruptcy

As I began looking for employment I was a little concerned about whether being open about my bankruptcy would go against me.

However, I decided to continue the policy of being completely honest I had adopted for the process, and face whatever consequences it would bring.

I made an appointment with the local job centre and applied for Jobseeker's Allowance in the meantime. My first experience at the Jobcentre Plus was less than positive. I was met by my 'personal adviser', who went through my skills and experience, noting that I had a degree in Business Law. He made a brief search for jobs that were available before recommending a delivery driver job at Tesco. And this was my personal adviser? I sat there bemused.

Over several weeks I applied for many varied roles - from multi-drop driver to executive officer. Each application I completed included the fact that I was an undischarged bankrupt. Most applications were not even acknowledged. For a few I was invited for interview and then heard nothing more.

After a couple of months a letter arrived from the Home Office. This informed me that I was invited for an interview for the post of executive officer. Deep down, this was a position that I really wanted, but as I was being overlooked for basic warehouse work I decide not to get my hopes up unduly. However, the interview went extremely well and I was informed at the end that they would be in touch.

A couple of weeks later I received a letter offering me the position, subject to pre-employment checks. As they already knew about my bankruptcy I was hopeful this wouldn't hinder my chances.

However, the pre-employment checks dragged on for nearly two months, until finally I received a letter advising me that I had been unsuccessful. I was hugely disappointed by this setback. If the British Government wouldn't give a bankrupt a second chance then who would?

I decided there and then that I would break my promise to myself about honesty, and refrain from mentioning my bankruptcy in future job applications. After all, it was not required.

The very same week I applied for a job on the night shift at a local hotel. I was interviewed twice, and then, within a fortnight of applying, I had achieved something that I found elusive as an 'honest bankrupt' in the previous eight months – I was back in employment.

As a result I would recommend that a discharged bankrupt does not disclose his or her status unless specifically asked to do so in the terms of the application.

2. Self-Employed

If you are self-employed bankruptcy will normally result in the closing down of your business and the dismissal of any employees. The trustee will claim all business assets, subject to certain exemptions. You will have to give the Official Receiver all of your accounting records, but remain responsible for completing all tax and VAT returns.

Your employees may be able to submit a claim to the National Insurance Fund for outstanding wages and holiday pay, payment in lieu of notice and redundancy. Any money owed that is not paid by the National Insurance Fund can be claimed by employees in the bankruptcy.

Continuing to trade

A bankrupt retains the right to earn a living from being self-employed, so you can begin to trade again should you so wish, even while you remain under a bankruptcy order. You must be careful to ensure that you abide by all the bankruptcy restrictions (see Chapter 20).

You are responsible for keeping accounting records for the business and for dealing with the appropriate tax and VAT requirements. If you meet the VAT registration requirements you will need to register again, you cannot continue to use your pre-bankruptcy VAT registration number.

Your business assets

Exempt property does not form part of the bankruptcy estate and is therefore not automatically available to the trustee to realise on behalf of the creditors. Property which should be treated as exempt includes any tools, books, vehicles and other equipment necessary for the personal use of the bankrupt to continue his or her business or vocation.

Stock or trading premises form part of the bankruptcy estate and therefore can be realised. Plant and machinery needed to carry out a business can be treated as exempt property where the bankrupt intends to continue to trade and the items are vital to allow the business to continue. Any such business assets are not exempt in circumstances where trading has ceased and is unlikely to restart.

In deciding whether to allow plant and machinery to be treated as exempt in the case of a bankrupt who continues to trade, the Official Receiver must take consideration of certain factors. These include viability of the business, its likely profitability, the ability to make payments under an income payments order, and the bankrupt's prospects of obtaining other employment. If the removal of such property will result in the bankrupt's loss of livelihood then the long term cost to the state of that consequence is also considered.

Surplus income

Where your earnings are more than sufficient for the reasonable domestic needs of you and your family, the trustee in bankruptcy may require you to contribute some of your surplus income under an income payments order, for a maximum of three years.

Trade-related registrations, licences and permissions

Your bankruptcy may affect any registrations, licences and permissions that you hold relating to your trade. You should seek clarification from the person who issued the registration or authority to establish whether it will remain in force, be cancelled or withdrawn as a result of your bankruptcy. Any value attached to these items may belong to the trustee.

27: Protecting Your Income

Income Payments Agreements and Income Payments Orders

One obvious benefit of bankruptcy to an individual is that payments to creditors immediately cease, as the estate becomes vested in the trustee in bankruptcy. This creates a situation where the bankrupt might have significant disposable income when previously there was none. Therefore the law aims to provide creditors with at least some part payment of that which they are owed.

This is achieved in the most part by selling off all assets and distributing the money between the creditors. In addition, where affordable, the trustee will seek an agreement with the bankrupt to make a contribution to the bankruptcy debts for up to three years.

The agreement can only be put in place during the period in which an individual is undischarged. If an agreement is not in place when discharged, no agreement can later be sought.

Under section 310A of the Insolvency Act 1986, the trustee has legal power to seek an income payments agreement (IPA). Although entered into voluntarily, the IPA is a written and formal binding agreement, with payments being made from any surplus income available after paying for certain living expenses.

Where an individual's personal circumstances change, either for the better or for worse, the IPA can be varied to ensure the payment is fair for both the bankrupt and his creditors.

If an individual fails to make the agreed payments, the trustee can apply to the court for an order suspending the discharge from bankruptcy, meaning that the individual would be subject to the restrictions of the bankruptcy order for longer. The trustee can apply to have the payments deducted directly from the individual's salary.

If the trustee is unable to reach an agreement with an individual regarding the amount of the payment, an application can be made to the court for an order enforcing the individual, or his/her employer, to make regular payments to the bankruptcy estate. The income payments order (IPO) is a court order, and therefore if the payments are not kept up the trustee can ask the court to make an order suspending the discharge from bankruptcy, or to take other legal action to recover the outstanding amounts.

The calculation

The court will not make an IPO where it would leave an individual without enough funds to cover the reasonable domestic needs of them and their family. 'Family' includes everyone living with the individual who is dependent upon them, e.g. adults who do not have an income. 'Reasonable domestic needs' are assessed by the trustee or the court by a thorough examination of the individual's circumstances.

The bankrupt's income and spending are recorded in the statement of affairs. The normal monthly expenses cover such things as rent, food, heating, lighting and clothing, amongst others, and the individual will be asked to provide proof of the income and expenditure listed in the form of payslips, utility bills, rent books, etc.

The trustee will assess the individual's monthly spending to decide whether, in the specific circumstances, it is reasonable. The reasonable domestic expenses are then deducted from the income to provide a figure showing the 'real disposable income' i.e. the money that is left over every month after all necessary expenses have been paid.

Normally the individual will have to use between 50 and 70 percent of their real disposable income each month for the IPA or IPO payments. If there is a large disposable income available then a greater percentage of it will generally be used. The trustee will not normally try to obtain an IPA or IPO where the main or only income of an individual is state benefits.

Where a bankrupt is self-employed, a fixed monthly payment figure may not be appropriate as income may be variable. The IPA will have to be tailored to the specific circumstances of the individual and should be reviewed regularly to allow for fluctuations in income.

What can be included within the 'reasonable monthly expenses?'

In addition to the normal monthly expenses previously listed, certain other expenses can be treated as part of an individual's domestic needs. Payments that can be included are: TV licence; TV and video hire; household insurance; car insurance and car tax; car breakdown cover; membership of any professional bodies required as part of the individual's employment; prescription; dental treatment; opticians; child maintenance or CSA payments; mobile phone, and dry cleaning. This list is not definitive, and other expenses could be included.

Payments which are not generally treated as allowable expenses, unless there are special circumstances, are those such as gym membership; additional pension contributions; private healthcare insurance; money for gambling, cigarettes or alcohol; satellite TV; excessive mortgage payments, and broadband internet costs (unless these are shown to be necessary for paid employment or education).

In assessing what is or is not a reasonable monthly expense the trustee will always consider the individual's view about what is a reasonable expense in their own particular circumstances. Modest allowances for family holidays and clothing are examples of expenses that have been considered reasonable in certain situations, along with allowances for after-school clubs where they are used to provide childcare whilst the parents are working.

An individual's income includes all payments received,

including those from self-employment, PAYE employment, benefits, working tax credit, and payments under a pension scheme.

The income details of an individual's partner are also required, as it is assumed that they also contribute to the household expenses. Details are also required of any payments received from other members of the household who contribute to the household expenses. Where an individual is unwilling to provide such information they will be unable to claim the full amount of all household expenses.

Duration of the IPO or IPA

An agreement or order normally runs for 3 years commencing on the date it is made. Thus it is likely to last beyond the period of bankruptcy.

Changes to income and expenditure

The trustee must be contacted immediately with the updated information, and the agreement or order may be changed to take account of the new change of circumstances. The trustee can decide to suspend the agreement until the financial situation improves.

Missed payments

If a payment is missed, the trustee will ask the individual for an explanation, and, if only a short-term problem, will arrange for the arrears to be made up over a short period. If the problem is longer term, the trustee will re-evaluate the situation and if he or she is satisfied that the IPA or IPO is no longer appropriate can suspend or reduce the repayments until such time as the situation improves.

When the situation improves, the individual has a duty to inform the trustee immediately so that the agreement or order can be restarted or increased. However, the term of the agreement is not extended, so the original end date of the agreement is still binding.

If one or more payments are missed and the trustee is not informed of any difficulties in making the payments, an application might be made to the court for an order suspending the individual's discharge from bankruptcy. The trustee can then take steps to recover any outstanding monies, which can include obtaining another bankruptcy order. When a payment is not made under an IPO, the individual is held in contempt and risks punishment by the court.

IPO's and the 'nil tax' code

If you pay tax under the PAYE system, HM Revenue and Customs will usually apply a 'nil tax' code to you for the rest of the tax year in which you were declared bankrupt. The effect of this is to instruct the individual's employer not to take any more income tax from their wages for the remainder of the tax year.

Because of the nil tax code there will be extra money in the individual's pay, and this money will form the basis of an IPA or IPO even where there is no other real disposable income. Therefore this may be the only amount payable, and as soon as the tax code changes the agreement or order will stop. If you have other real disposable income the IPA or IPO will reduce when your tax code changes.

28: Your Pension

When considering how bankruptcy will affect your pension arrangements it is necessary to identify what pensions you have or will be entitled to in the future. There are four types:

- **State pension** – includes any payment from the State Second Pension (S2P – formerly known as SERPS)
- **Occupational pension** – a scheme set up by an employer to provide members with retirement and death benefits
- **Personal pension plan** – a personal pension policy taken out with an insurance company to pay benefits in later life
- **Group personal pension** – a personal pension policy taken out with a pension provider, usually negotiated on favourable rates and terms by an employer or trade association

Duties towards your trustee in bankruptcy

As a bankrupt you have a duty to co-operate with and provide all the information requested by your trustee. The trustee will require details of all pensions including the name of any occupational pension scheme which you, and your past and present employer acting on your behalf, have contributed to. Evidence will also be required detailing what benefit you receive or will receive under any occupational pension scheme and how much has been contributed to them, particularly in the previous two years.

Your trustee will also request the policy details for all personal pension plans you have begun. Additionally, where you are receiving a pension, your trustee will want to know the amount of your regular benefits and the dates and amounts of any lump sums you have received.

The effect of bankruptcy on your pension

If your bankruptcy petition was presented on or after 29 May 2000, all pension schemes that have been approved by HM Revenue and Customs remain outside a bankrupt's estate, and therefore cannot be claimed by the trustee.

Approved pension schemes

The most common approved arrangements are personal pension schemes approved by HM Revenue and Customs for tax purposes; pension schemes registered under Section 153 of the Finance Act 2004; retirement annuity contracts, and stakeholder pensions.

The trustee in bankruptcy will write to your pension provider to obtain confirmation if there is any doubt as to whether your pension scheme is approved. Where the trustee is satisfied that your pension is in an approved arrangement he or she will write to you and your pension provider to confirm that the pension does not form part of the bankruptcy estate.

Unapproved schemes

If your pension scheme is unapproved, it may still be possible to exclude it from your bankruptcy estate by applying to the court for an exclusion order or by making a qualifying agreement with your trustee. Where the pension policy does form part of your bankruptcy estate, the trustee can claim both the lump sum and regular payments even after your discharge from bankruptcy. In certain circumstances, it may be possible for you to buy back your interest in the pension policy from the trustee.

Pension payments received whilst bankrupt

If you receive payments from a pension before your discharge from bankruptcy, the payments can be included in the calculation for an income payments order, even if the trustee cannot claim your pension or any part of it.

State pensions

Neither the state pension, nor any payments from the State Second Pension (S2P), form part of the bankruptcy estate.

Pension contributions whilst bankrupt

Pension contributions can continue to be made under your existing pension arrangements or under new pension arrangements made after the bankruptcy order.

Where your trustee claims all or part of your pension benefits it may not be advisable to continue making payments, as you may not receive the full benefit of them. Further clarification should be sought from your pension provider or an independent financial adviser.

Effect of death during bankruptcy

If an individual dies before the date of their discharge from bankruptcy, the trustee can claim the death benefit if the pension scheme does not nominate a beneficiary, or class of beneficiary.

Bankruptcy petitions presented before 29 May 2000

If your bankruptcy petition was presented before 29 May 2000, your trustee may claim all or part of your pension, whether you are receiving it already or it is due in the future.

29: Securing Early Discharge

You will usually be discharged from bankruptcy on the first anniversary of your bankruptcy order. However, if the Official Receiver concludes his or her enquiries into your affairs, he or she may file a notice of early discharge in court.

Although many people are discharged early from the restrictions imposed by bankruptcy, it is worth noting that there is no automatic right to receive an early discharge. Such a decision is at the discretion of your Official Receiver.

Timescales

The Official Receiver will usually compile a report to your creditors within eight weeks of the bankruptcy order, providing all investigations have been satisfactorily completed. The more open, honest and co-operative you are the sooner it will happen.

Three months after the report has been issued, the Official Receiver will review your file. If it is concluded that there are no other matters in the bankruptcy that require further investigation then the Official Receiver will begin the early discharge process.

He will write to your creditors and your trustee (where appointed) advising them of the intention to file notice of early discharge. Your creditors have twenty-eight-days to lodge objections. If an objection necessitates further investigation of your affairs the early discharge process will be stopped. If no objections are received, or if any such objections are resolved, the Official Receiver will then send notice of early discharge to the court. You will receive a copy of the notice confirming your date of discharge, stamped by the court.

Keeping the Official Receiver and trustee updated

It is very much in your interests that both the Official Receiver and your trustee (where appointed) are kept up-to-date with your contact and address details, as you will be sent notification of your discharge when it occurs.

In my own case, prior to the anniversary of my bankruptcy order I called the Official Receiver's office to confirm when I would receive my automatic discharge. The Official Receiver's office advised that I had already been discharged by the court some two months earlier – notification had been sent but it had gone to my previous address. I had been discharged from bankruptcy for two months without knowing it.

This was despite the fact that I had called the Official Receiver's office some six months into my bankruptcy to enquire whether I might be eligible for early discharge. I was told that in some circumstances early discharge does occur, but it would not be happening in my case.

Consequently it is worthwhile contacting the Official Receiver's office at regular intervals, maybe every month or so, to check on their progress and to push for your early discharge. Some individuals have been discharged within six months of the bankruptcy order being made.

The circumstances of each individual bankruptcy are unique, and so what happens in your own case will depend on several variables, including the discretion and goodwill of the civil servants involved. Consequently, by taking ownership of your situation, you could be discharged a good deal earlier than anticipated, allowing you to get on with your life free from the restrictions of bankruptcy.

Part V: After You Are Discharged

30: The Process and Effects of Discharge

Under the Enterprise Act 2002, which came into effect in April 2004, an automatic discharge from bankruptcy is usually made after one year for anyone who has not been made bankrupt within the last 15 years or has not been made criminally bankrupt.

On discharge, the restrictions of bankruptcy are taken away, and you are released from the debts that were included in your bankruptcy. Certain debts that cannot be included in bankruptcy proceedings are not affected by your discharge and you remain liable for their repayment (see *The Effects of Discharge*, below).

Discharge will usually occur automatically, even where no payments have been made to your creditors; you are still making payments under an income payments agreement, or where some of your assets have not yet been sold.

Although the Official Receiver can apply to the court for a bankruptcy restrictions order, which will extend the restrictions after discharge, this will not affect the discharge of your debts.

You will usually be discharged after twelve months, on the anniversary of the bankruptcy order. However, you could find yourself discharged even sooner. When the Official Receiver has completed enquiries into your affairs he or she may file a notice of early discharge in court. It is effective immediately.

- **Bankruptcies made prior to 1 April 2004**

If it was your first bankruptcy you should have been discharged automatically on 1 April 2005. Alternatively, if you expected your discharge date to be before 1 April 2005, you should have been discharged on the earlier date.

If you were an undischarged bankrupt at any time during the fifteen years before the current bankruptcy (unless the previous bankruptcy was annulled), your discharge should have automatically occurred on 1 April 2009.

If your discharge was suspended prior to 1 April 2004, you should contact your Official Receiver for information.

- **Do I need a certificate of discharge?**

You can obtain, free of charge, a letter from your Official Receiver confirming the date of your discharge. This letter is useful when having to show banks, building societies, creditors and credit reference agencies written confirmation of your discharge. Many companies are obliged to ask for proof to ensure that you have been freed from the restrictions of bankruptcy and are not attempting to conceal anything from the Official Receiver or trustee.

In my experience, most companies will automatically ask for a certificate of discharge. The certificate entails a fee of £60. So writing to your Official Receiver to obtain a letter confirming your date of discharge can save you this additional expense. Most companies are happy to accept this letter in place of the certificate.

If it is necessary to obtain a certificate of discharge you should write to the court dealing with it no sooner than two weeks before your discharge date. You must provide your name, address and court number, so that the court can confirm with the Official Receiver that you are entitled to automatic discharge. Once confirmed the certificate should be received within four weeks.

If you require the Official Receiver to advertise your discharge you will pay the costs of the advertising in advance.

- **Cancellation of automatic discharge**

You will not be automatically discharged from your bankruptcy if your discharge period has been suspended (e.g. if you failed to co-operate with the Official Receiver or trustee), or if you are subject to a criminal bankruptcy order.

148

The Effects of Discharge

Once discharged you are released from most debts which you incurred before the bankruptcy order. However, there are certain types of debt that discharge does not release you from. These include:
- non-provable debts (see Chapter 22)
- debt arising from fraudulent conduct or certain other crimes
- debts incurred after the date of the bankruptcy order
- outstanding student loans (you may still have to repay your student loan if you were made bankrupt before 1st of September 2004. The Official Receiver can provide further clarification).

• **Assets owned or obtained before your discharge** – any of your assets that the Official Receiver or trustee held or claimed during your bankruptcy remain under the control of the Official Receiver or trustee, and generally are not returned upon discharge. It could be some time after your discharge before all of your assets are finally dealt with. You must inform the Official Receiver of any assets you obtain after the trustee has finished dealing with your case but *before* you are discharged. You will usually be allowed to keep all assets acquired *after* your discharge.

• **Mortgage payments** – all secured creditors (those lenders who hold security such as a mortgage) retain the right to recover or enforce their security if your repayments are not met.

• **Your home** – your interest in your home may be returned to you if no action has been taken by the trustee within a certain period, usually three years from the date of the bankruptcy order.

• **Income payments agreement** – where you are making payments under an income payments agreement or order you must continue to make these payments as agreed after your discharge.

• **Creditor advertisement** – where your trustee is making a payment to your creditors he or she may place an advertisement about your bankruptcy in a newspaper asking creditors to submit their claims. Where it takes a trustee a long time to deal with an asset, the advertisement may appear several years after the bankruptcy order.

• **Your business** – after you have been discharged you are free to carry on a business without the restrictions that applied during your bankruptcy. You are able to act as a director of a limited company or be involved in its management – unless you are subject to a bankruptcy restrictions order or separate disqualification order.

• **Obtaining credit** – you can also obtain credit without having to mention your bankruptcy unless you are specifically asked to do so, or you are the subject of a bankruptcy restrictions order.

• **Continued co-operation** – you must continue to co-operate with the Official Receiver and/or trustee even after your discharge, e.g. by providing any requested information. Failure to do so could make you liable to contempt of court.

Public records

• **Individual Insolvency Register** – the register, maintained by the Insolvency Service, contains records of bankruptcy orders and individual voluntary arrangements in England and Wales. Your bankruptcy details will remain on the register for three months after the date of your discharge.

• **H M Land Registry** – bankruptcy details remain on the register for five years. Although discharge has no effect on this, you can apply to the court to have the entries removed. Restriction notices may also have been registered against the title to the property. Where the interest in your home is returned, the trustee will notify the Chief Land Registrar that it is no longer part of your bankruptcy estate.

• **Credit reference agencies** – you may have to provide separate information to the credit reference agencies in order for them to update their records (see Chapter 32).

31: Distribution of the Bankruptcy Estate

After realising the assets of a bankrupt the trustee will distribute the money raised in accordance with an order of priority set out in insolvency law.

The expenses of the bankruptcy

These are also paid out in a set order of priority, and include:

• expenses incurred in preserving, realising or getting in the assets of the bankrupt

• fees and remuneration which are payable to the Official Receiver and the Secretary of State. The trustee has to pay all money realised into an Insolvency Services Account held at the Bank of England. A 'Secretary of State fee' (also known as an 'ad valorem' fee) is calculated as a percentage of the amount.

• the costs of the petitioner

• any disbursements made by the trustee

• the payment of anyone employed by the trustee to provide services in the bankruptcy

• the payment of the trustee

• any capital gains tax due on increases in the value of assets since the date of the bankruptcy order

Claims of preferential creditors

These are the first creditors to get paid, and include any claims by employees for unpaid wages and holiday pay and certain contributions to occupational pension schemes. Where insufficient money is realised to pay these creditors in full, the money that is realised is paid to them in proportion to the amount they are owed.

Debts which are neither preferential nor postponed

Such debts are usually referred to as debts of unsecured creditors, and include trade and expense creditors. Again if there is insufficient money realised to pay them in full they will each be paid in proportion to the amount that they are owed. This is referred to as a dividend of pence in the pound, e.g. payment of half of that which they were owed would equate to a dividend of 50 pence in the pound.

Interest of debts

Where preferential and unsecured creditor debts are paid in full they are also entitled to interest on the amounts dating from the date of the bankruptcy order.

Debts to postponed creditors

Such debts include money owed to a person who was a spouse of the bankrupt at the date of the bankruptcy order.

Surplus

If a surplus remains after paying in full all the expenses of the bankruptcy, all debts of the bankrupt and interest on the debts, then this money is returned to the bankrupt.

The distribution of my own bankruptcy estate

Fourteen months after being declared bankrupt, and some five months receiving early discharge, I received a copy of the final report issued to creditors from a business recovery and insolvency firm acting on behalf of my trustee. It advised me of the date of the final meeting of my creditors and confirmed I was not required to attend.

The final analysis of my own bankruptcy made interesting reading. The sale of assets raised over £18,000, of which the Official Receiver received £1,300. The Secretary of State fee was £2,700.

Over £2,000 was irrecoverable VAT. £2,200 went on legal fees. The trustee's fee was £15,400. Less than £10,000 remained to make this payment, so there was no dividend remaining to pay any class of creditor.

As such it is little surprise that the vast majority of personal bankruptcies are petitioned by the debtor rather than the creditor. In most cases the creditors will have very little, if anything, to gain after all other expenses relating to the bankruptcy have been paid. In my case over £18,000 came a long way short of even covering the expenses of administering the bankruptcy.

32: Repairing Your Credit Rating

Credit reference agencies

The three main consumer credit reference agencies in the UK are Experian, Equifax and Call Credit. They provide lenders with information about potential borrowers, to enable lending decisions.

They hold information about most adults in the UK, including previous credit history, which is known as your *credit reference file* or *credit report*. If personal information held about you is incorrect or out-of-date, it could lead to you being unfairly refused credit and under the Data Protection Act 1998 you have the right to ask for a copy and correct any incorrect information.

You can obtain a copy of your credit report online or by post directly from the credit reference agency for a payment of £2. You should also provide the following information:

- your full name and any other names you have been known by, e.g. your maiden name,
- your full address including postcode, any addresses where you have lived over the past six years,
- your date of birth.

The credit reference agency has seven working days to send you your file after receiving your application and fee.

Experian can be contacted on 0844 481 8000 or on its website, www.experian.co.uk.

Equifax are available on 0870 010 0583 or online at www.equifax.co.uk.

Call Credit can be reached on 0870 060 1414, with further information at www.callcredit.co.uk.

The benefits of ensuring your credit files are accurate

Once each account is marked as *settled* or *satisfied* the account is correctly closed with the creditor or debt collection agency. This will prevent any possible hassle from previous creditors in the future. There have been instances where debt collectors have been incorrectly chasing debt years after a bankruptcy order due to lack of such updating.

Additionally, where inaccurate information is held, creditors might not close the account for several years, meaning that your credit reference file may be affected much longer than the standard six years.

As each account is marked as settled your credit score will improve, allowing you to rebuild your financial standing more quickly.

Checking the information on your credit file

A bankruptcy will stay on your credit reference file for six years from the date of your bankruptcy order. You should ensure that the date of your discharge from bankruptcy is shown correctly. If it is not, or is incorrect, you should contact the credit reference agency to inform them of the correct details and supply associated proof. This can be either a certificate of discharge or a letter from your Official Receiver confirming the date of your discharge. Such a letter can be obtained free of charge from your Official Receiver.

Accounts included in your bankruptcy may show on your credit report as being in default. The date of default should be no later than the date of the bankruptcy order. Details of your bankruptcy will automatically be removed from your credit reference file on the sixth anniversary. If any defaults are dated after the date of the bankruptcy order they will stay on your report longer than your bankruptcy, adversely affecting your credit rating beyond the standard six year period.

If the information on your credit report is wrong you can write to the lender or the credit reference agency. A credit reference agency will normally need to contact the lender to investigate your complaint, therefore it may be quicker for you to contact the lender directly.

Writing to the lender

Provide your full name and address along with any relevant account or reference numbers to help them find your information. You should also explain what information you think is wrong and why, and provide any proof you have to show this. The lender should be allowed a reasonable time to investigate the problem and reply – usually twenty-eight days. If you do not receive a response you should send a follow-up letter, keeping copies of all letters than you send.

Writing to the credit reference agency

Provide your full name and address and your credit reference file number. Explain what information you think is wrong and why and provide any proof you have. Also keep a copy of the letter.

By law the agency must tell you within twenty-eight days if it has removed the entry, amended the entry, or taken no action.

Taking your complaint to the Information Commissioner

If, after writing to the lender or credit reference agency, the information is still incorrect you may wish to contact the Information Commissioner, who has responsibility for enforcing the Data Protection Act.

You should write to the Information Commissioner giving details of your full name and address, explaining what you think is wrong and why. Enclose copies of the letters sent to or received from the lender or agency, along with any proof you have to show why the information is wrong.

The Information Commissioner will consider the information you provide, and may decide to contact the lender or credit reference agency for their comments, before deciding if any action is appropriate.

The Information Commissioner's Office can be contacted by telephone on 0845 630 6060, with further information available online at www.ico.gov.uk.

Using credit repair companies

Credit repair companies will charge a fee for carrying out work that you can undertake yourself, i.e. by getting the information held on your credit report updated to help improve your credit rating. By taking the steps to update the information yourself you can save any unnecessary additional expense, and probably get it completed much quicker.

Eligibility for further credit

When deciding whether to give you credit, lenders such as banks and loan companies want to be confident that you will repay the money they lend. To help them do this they will look at the information held by the credit reference agencies. Remember that details of your bankruptcy will appear on your credit reference file for six years after the date of your bankruptcy order.

Higher risk means higher rates

The greater a risk you are considered, the less likely a bank or building society will be to agree any lending. Where there is a bankruptcy restrictions order in place it may be even more difficult. Also, where a lender is willing to agree credit, it is likely that you will be charged a higher than usual rate of interest to cover the perceived risk involved.

That being said there are today a number of companies who specialise in providing credit to those with poor credit histories, including those who have been through bankruptcy.

Secured borrowing such as a mortgage is probably amongst the least difficult of facilities for a discharged bankrupt to obtain, as it is secured against a property.

Banks also tend to look more favourably on applications if an unforeseen circumstance caused the bankruptcy, e.g. illness or unemployment, and where you are able to show that you are now in better shape. Again, interest charged on the amount borrowed is likely to be higher than that offered to borrowers without poor credit ratings.

33: Budgeting for a Debt-Free Future

The benefits of budgeting

A personal budget provides an accurate picture of your financial position, helping to highlight where spending habits can be changed, putting you on the path to a worry-free financial future.

Taking the time to prepare an accurate budget will provide benefits for you and your family in the long term by ensuring that basic needs are met and helping to avoid impulse spending.

A budget will help alleviate any stress you may otherwise be experiencing, and provide for some contingency in the case of a worst case scenario, e.g. redundancy. It will also allow you to build up savings to cover for any unexpected emergencies.

Your budget should be viewed as a tool for empowerment, allowing you the ability to take control of your finances. Staying on budget will take commitment, but by doing so you are sure to reap the benefits.

Drawing up your budget

Start by dividing a blank sheet of paper into two columns.

In the left-hand column, list details of all monthly income: earnings; interest on savings or investments; benefits or tax credits; rent received from lodgers etc. If you have joint finances, include your partner's income.

In the right-hand column, detail all of your monthly expenditure. Be thorough. By writing everything down you will more easily identify any unnecessary spending:

1. **Essential commitments** – your rent or mortgage payments; council tax; utility bills; insurances, including life insurance; pension contributions; maintenance payments; regular car expenses (insurance, MOT and tax); credit cards; loans; hire purchase; second mortgage repayments; any child maintenance. Add up the costs so you have a sub-total for your essential expenditure.

2. **Everyday expenses** – all daily expenditure, including food bills, public transport costs, petrol, cigarettes, alcohol, entertainment, eating out and so on. List any monies spent on leisure activities. If you have children, include the costs of their care plus clothes and toys etc. If you have pets, you should also list expenditure for their food, vet's fees and so on. Add up the costs to provide your sub-total for everyday expenditure.

3. **Occasional expenses** – this part of the budget is crucial, and yet is often overlooked. Some payments don't occur every month and are not planned, e.g. car repairs, Christmas and birthday presents, holiday expenses. Over time money may be required for getting the central heating boiler fixed, paying a dentist bill, purchasing a new mobile phone or laptop etc.

List everything you can think of. Add it all up (some may have to be estimated), then divide by twelve. This is the amount to include in the occasional expenses budget.

It is very helpful to open up a savings account specifically to fund these expenses. Deposit the monthly amount of your occasional expenses in that account each month, e.g. if your irregular expenses total £2,400 for the year, you would deposit £200 per month into this account. Then, whenever such an expense comes up, you can pay for it out of this account.

Now add the three sub-totals together to calculate your grand expenses total. Then deduct this amount from your total income figure to give you the balance.

Surplus income

If the balance indicates a surplus each month, the wise option is to put the excess money into savings or investments, rather than leaving it in your bank account where it may prove tempting.

Building up savings for emergencies is vital (at least three months' income as a minimum). And you may want to save for a car, house deposit or other large purchase. Excess funds can also be used towards pensions, mortgage overpayments, or to clear debts.

Making cutbacks

If you have little or no surplus income it is imperative that you think carefully about how to make cut-backs on your spending whilst taking all possible steps to boost your income.

Amending your shopping habits

- Much of people's day-to-day spending is habitual. Rather than purchasing sandwiches, snacks and drinks at cafes make your own from food bought at more economical supermarket prices.
- Shop around at discount outlets for better deals. Buy generic brands and look to buy in bulk where appropriate.
- Use cash for purchases; refrain from obtaining credit to finance your lifestyle. If you don't have the money in your pocket to make the purchase then you really cannot afford it.
- If you would like the flexibility to purchase products and services as you would with a debit or credit card then get a pre-paid card. As you can only spend the amount that has been pre-loaded on to the card there is no risk of running into debt.
- Don't impulse buy. If you see something tempting, go home and think it over. It is unlikely you will return to buy.
- Don't purchase an item just because it is in a sale. When you do so you are not making savings, but spending unnecessarily.
- Have the confidence to haggle over prices, especially when paying by cash.

Making lifestyle changes

- Ensure you conduct your bank account in a proper manner. The way you operate your accounts from now on must be exemplary if you are going to avoid problems, charges and have further lending agreed.
- Find out what benefits or tax credits are available. You could also consider asking for extra hours at work.
- Make use of the resources available at your local library; including books, CD's, videos, newspapers and magazines.
- Make your car economical to run by ensuring it is serviced, checked by you (oil, water, tyres) regularly, and is only used when necessary.
- Send e-mails rather than making long-distance calls.
- Make use of Freeview rather than paying for premium subscriptions.
- Be creative - go for a walks, rent videos, watch local sports. The possibilities are limited only by your imagination.

Keep it under review

You should review your budget periodically as your income and outgoings fluctuate. Keep making adjustments. It is a process, and the more you do it the easier it becomes. Managing your finances online will provide closer control of your expenditure.

Avoiding future temptation

There might remain an underlying cause to the problems that resulted in your bankruptcy, e.g. being a compulsive debtor or gambler. As such you should take advantage of the free support services available to help you deal with the root cause of the issue and find a solution:

- **Debtors Anonymous** is a group for people who wish to stop using any form of unsecured debt. Members share their experiences on recovery from compulsive indebtedness, with help and support available free of charge. For further information you can telephone them on 0207 1177 533 or visit their website at www.debtorsanonymous.org.uk.

• **Gamblers Anonymous** is a group who have joined together to do something about their own gambling problem, and to help other compulsive gamblers do the same. Further information is available online at www.gamblersanonymous.co.uk or on 0207 384 3040.

Each person's own preferences, habits and lifestyle are different. There is no 'one size fits all' solution to keeping out of financial trouble. It will be a case of trial and error, making adjustments that allow you to continue to enjoy life, whilst having the restraint and control to ensure you are not faced with measures as drastic as bankruptcy in the future.

34: No Regrets

After being trapped beneath a huge financial burden for a long period of time and struggling to see a way out, the eventual realisation you are debt-free again is truly an exhilarating experience.

Bankruptcy can foster unhelpful and unwarranted feelings of guilt and shame, and maybe even some degree of foolishness. An impending financial meltdown brings with it many associated demons, not least dark days filled with worry and despair, culminating in months or even years littered with sleepless nights.

Having to avoid telephone calls and being swamped with demands for money can take a massive toll on a person's spirit and self-esteem. Making any kind of plans for the future can also be incredibly difficult when your immediate focus is on how you are going to make it through the next month.

The truth is that the benefits of becoming bankrupt by far and away outweigh any of the negativity or perceived stigma. Everyone makes mistakes, and everybody must be allowed the opportunity to recover from their difficulties and start afresh.

The financial lessons learned as a result of going through the bankruptcy process will stay with you for the rest of your life. You will banish those sleepless nights for good, put a stop to creditor phone calls and letters, eliminate endless bank charges and interest payments, and have free time to get on with living your life.

The only regret that people seem to share is that they didn't take the plunge and opt for bankruptcy sooner, avoiding extra stress and suffering. Bankruptcy is frequently referred to by those who have been through it as 'the best thing I ever did'. Life truly can be transformed.

Don't get me wrong, personal insolvency is far from a bed of roses. There are long term consequences, and as such bankruptcy is something that should not be entered into lightly. You should always seek professional help and make sure you fully understand all of the implications for you and your family. But nothing worthwhile came easily and without sacrifice.

One of the stark realities that bankruptcy exposes is the necessity to begin living within your means, curbing any excessive spending habits. Charles Dickens famously encapsulated the formula for financial peace of mind in David Copperfield:

Annual income twenty pounds, annual expenditure nineteen six, result happiness. Annual income twenty pounds, annual expenditure twenty pound ought and six, result misery.

It is often said there is a fine line between success and failure, and nowhere is this statement truer than in relation to your own personal finances.

Simple changes like spending cash again, rather than using plastic, become empowering actions. Knowing that the cash in your hand is one hundred percent yours is a gratifying feeling. You will become an expert at budgeting, knowing exactly how much income you receive against the amount of outgoings you have.

Living within your means allows amounts of money, no matter how small, to be saved, increasing your net worth and providing a useful resource should you have the misfortune to suffer an unexpected mishap. Regaining control of your financial future allows you to face such challenges with a greater degree of confidence.

Out of great adversity, positive lifestyle changes occur. The relief in stress levels is without comparison. It is an amazing feeling to wake up each morning free from the heavy burden of debt that once weighed upon you. After years of struggling in vain to keep your head above water, you will experience a notable improvement in your health as you feel more relaxed and assured, safe in the knowledge that you now have the skills and resources to combat any future financial difficulties that might head your way.

Surviving bankruptcy provides a tremendous boost to self-confidence. When you reshape your life after suffering extreme financial hardship, you realise that the material possessions you had to give up are not as important as they seemed.

The joy that emanates from the experience comes in the realisation that the truly valuable items you possess – your spirit, determination and sense of humour – are commodities that can never be taken away. Control of your life is now fully back in your hands, now you have completed a journey that has armed you with some of the most useful lessons you can ever learn.

Part VI: Glossary

This glossary is for general guidance only; many of the terms have a specific technical meaning in certain contexts which are not necessarily covered within this book.

Administration order – an order made in a county court to arrange and administer the payment of debts by an individual.

Annulment – cancellation.

Assets – anything belonging to the debtor that may be used to pay off debts.

Bankrupt – an individual against whom a bankruptcy order has been made by the court.

Bankruptcy – the process of dealing with the estate of a bankrupt.

Bankruptcy Restriction Notice – a notice entered at the Land Registry on any property involved in a bankruptcy.

Bankruptcy order – a court order making an individual bankrupt.

Bankruptcy petition – a request made to the court for a debtor to be made bankrupt.

Bankruptcy restrictions order or undertaking (BRO/BRU) – a procedure whereby the restrictions of bankruptcy continue to apply to a dishonest or culpable bankrupt after discharge, for between two to fifteen years.

Beneficial Interest – a right to, or share in, a property (see also **Interest**).

169

Centre of main interest (COMI) – Place where most transaction occurs (for a business), or where an individual lives or works.

Charge – a security interest taken over property by a creditor to protect against non-payment of a debt, e.g. a mortgage.

Charging order – an order made by the court giving the trustee a legal charge on the bankrupt's property for the amount owed.

Creditor – someone owed money by a bankrupt.

Creditors' committee – a committee representing the interests of all creditors in supervising the activities of a trustee in bankruptcy.

Debt Management Plan (DMP) – an informal arrangement negotiated with creditors by an independent company.

Debt Relief Order (DRO) – An alternative to bankruptcy introduced in 2009, for small-scale debts.

Debtor – someone who owes money.

Debts – money owed.

Discharge – being freed from bankruptcy.

Director – a person conducting the affairs of a company.

Dividend – a sum distributed to unsecured creditors.

Estate – assets or property of the bankrupt which the trustee can deal with to pay the creditors.

Excess Value – the value of property that could be sold and replaced by one of lower cost.

Fast Track Voluntary Arrangement (FTVA) – a voluntary agreement with creditors to pay all or part of the money owed, which can only be entered into after being made bankrupt.

Income payments agreement (IPA) – a written agreement where the bankrupt voluntarily agrees to pay the trustee part of his or her income for an agreed period.

Income payments order (IPO) – where the court orders the bankrupt to pay part of their income to the trustee for a period.

Individual voluntary arrangement (IVA) – a voluntary arrangement for an individual where a compromise scheme for satisfying debts is put forward to creditors.

Insolvency – being unable to pay debts as and when they are due.

Insolvency Act 1986 – primary legislation governing insolvency law.

Insolvency practitioner – an authorised person specialising in insolvency, usually an accountant or solicitor.

Insolvency Services Account – an account maintained at the Bank of England through which bankruptcy funds must be passed.

Interest – a right to, or share in, a property (also bank interest).

Interim order – precludes bankruptcy and other legal proceedings whilst in force.

Jurisdiction – the authority of a court to deal with legal proceedings.

Legal charge – a form of security to ensure payment of a debt.

Mortgage – the transfer of an interest in land or other property by way of security, with the express or implied condition that the asset shall be re-conveyed to the debtor when the sum secured has been paid.

Nil Tax Code – a tax code applied to bankrupts, but also for other reasons, such as overpayments in previous years.

Nominee – an insolvency practitioner who carries out the preparatory work for a voluntary arrangement.

Non-provable debt – debt which is not included in the bankruptcy proceedings. An individual remains liable for such debt regardless of his or her bankruptcy.

Official Receiver – a civil servant (and officer of the court) employed by The Insolvency Service, which deals with bankruptcies.

Petition – a formal application made to a court.

Preference – a payment or other transaction made by an individual which places a creditor in a better position than they would otherwise have been.

Preferential creditor – a creditor entitled to receive certain payments in priority to floating charge holders and other unsecured creditors.

Public examination – where the Official Receiver questions the bankrupt in open court.

Realise – to sell or dispose of an asset to raise money.

Secured creditor – a creditor holding security, such as a mortgage.

Security – a charge or mortgage over assets taken to secure the payment of a debt. Where the debt is not paid, the lender has a right to sell the charged assets.

Statement of affairs – a document completed by a bankrupt, and sworn under oath, stating the assets and giving details of debts and creditors.

Transaction at an undervalue – either a gift or a transaction in which the consideration received is significantly less than that given.

Trustee - either the Official Receiver or an insolvency practitioner who takes control of the assets of a bankrupt.

Unsecured creditor – a creditor who does not hold any security for money owed.

Unsecured debt – a debt owed to an unsecured creditor.

YOUR NOTES
a place for useful contacts, numbers and addresses